Gas Station Dick Pills

And Other American Dreams

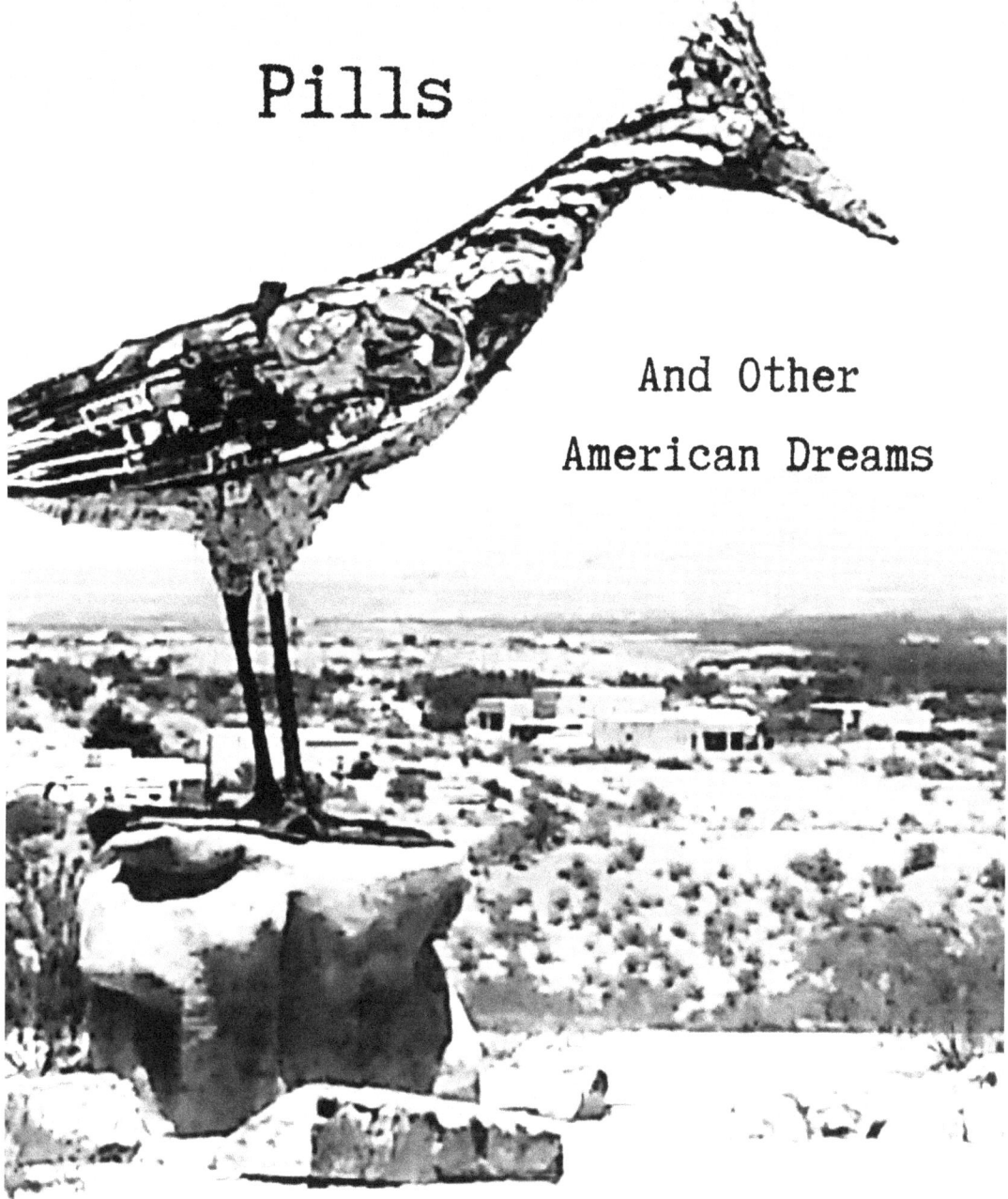

Cover Image and
Title Page Image: Recycled Roadrunner Sculpture
                   by Olin Calk
                   Las Cruces New Mexico

                   Photo, editing and layout by Terry Blade

Back Cover Image: J Nyhel, Lethal Dose Images
                   Suspension by Life Suspended

Interior Graphics: Terry Blade (see notes)

Chest Suspension Image: Screenshot from a video shot by
                         Russ Broty, filtered and cropped by
                         Terry Blade
                         Suspension by Life Suspended

[another American dream]
[another american dream] A Bitter Taste
[another american dream] i believed i knew what my life was about...
Praise for your collarbones
My gender is murder...
were previously published digitally in the anthology
The Paradox Of Constriction by Crooked Treehouse Press

[this is not a dream] [in the midst of] [Fissure], and
How [The American Dream]
Tried to Skullfuck Me on Public Alley Nine-Oh-Nine
were previously published digitally in the anthology
 I Came Back From The Dead And Couldn't Stop Talking
 by Crooked Treehouse Press

Claimer

People and beings in this book are real humans, others, non-corporeal, composites, long dead, long dead to me or exist as some combination of these attributes.

If you see yourself in these words, that is most likely in your own mind. Don't make it someone else's problem. Be as butthurt as you want, but I'm not changing my words.

These are my words, except where I have used quotes. I have taken inspiration from musicians, writers, and poets, from works that have had an influence on me. I have attempted to cite these either with the poem or in the notes. The characters of Dale Gribble, Peggy Hill, Buckley, and Lucifer are obviously not my own creation but I have portrayed them through the lens of my own experiences, and perceptions.

On Dreams

I like to let my poetry do the talking, but there are things that perhaps I should say. It's easy to sell dreams to some people who have lived in desperation. And the dream-sellers themselves are often the ones who create those desperate conditions.

I exist because my grandparents got the fuck out. Each side of my family came from different places, different countries, but the results were the same. Those who stayed behind were murdered. The family that I knew was very small. If you are a Holocaust denier, get the fuck out of my book. Same goes for followers of Netanyahu. We should endeavor not to become the evil that we have survived.

In America the pressure to fit in was (and is) overwhelming. I think of the carrot and the stick. Difference was brutally punished. On the other hand, comfort was not truly attainable for immigrants or their children. And I have to be particular here, and say Jewish immigrants, and their children because that is who I come from, and how I was brought up. While there are some universal aspects to immigrant experiences, there are many that are specific to each individual group.

Please understand that I was born on the heels of the House Un-American Activities Committee. Queerness, Jewishness, and Communism were all conflated, and vigorously attacked.

Being a trans kid who was self-aware from a very young age was extremely painful and confusing. The words and ideas used today did not exist back around 1960. I just went to school, lined up with the girls, and tried to tell people who I was. I learned extremely quickly not to do that. I lived an utterly hopeless life. The more I tried to be myself, the worse things were for me. And the hits came from every direction. There was no safe place to be me, and definitely not at home. There's no real way to heal these wounds, to change the past. My only hope is that we somehow make things better in the future, and that we don't lose the understandings that we've gained.

The Lands That I Know Most Well

The lands that I've wandered for about one third of my life, and the lands where I lived most of the rest of my life are commonly called America. These lands were, and are still lived in, and walked upon, by people who were here long ages before my family arrived. They were here before that name existed, before the dreams associated with it were ever sold.

For
The Wanderers
The Weirdos
And
The Queers
With All The Love I Can Muster

Table Of Discontent, Made Glorious

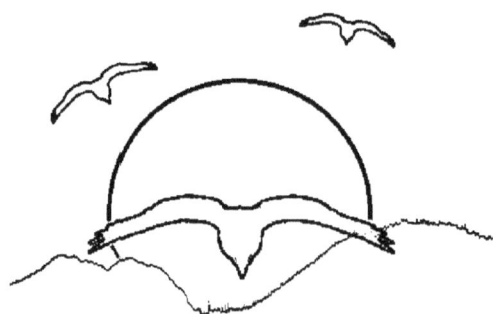

[another american dream]*

Maybe I need to get   some of that   gas station dick
Boy-Girl   Girl-Boy   Beats me
Chemically enhanced   like some days I care
Like some days my lust is an overstuffed
Coffee ice cream sandwich rising to my waiting lips
At the counter strewn with turbo lighters   nebulous nostrums
And wrinkled bags of crispy chicharrones
Like a pig by any name   can be me   like some days I care
And others   I drag my feet through dog day shadowed streets
And alleyways echo as I
Churn washed out graytop   into gravel of
My fevered american dreamless trance
This is how   to interstate
This is how any hustle is likely to suck a person in   lifeless
And gasping for a bit of breathing room   buying little mercies
With whatever lines the bottom of a pocket the bottom of a fifth
When I hit the bottom of that barrel
A sickening bounce into   something
Uncertain sequence of infinite migraine sunrise
Shuddering hand grips steaming styrofoam cup
Tight V of my fingers caressing
A factory rolled cylinder   mass produced
Curl of personal smokestack
The way I sit watching ash and slag grow
Over me   cause I spit in the devil's eye one too many times
And   there's those lips of mine again
Waiting
Always waiting
For another little taste of mercy

*After Doomtree's song *Little Mercy*

1

Ricochet (for the vagabonds)

Are steel wheels even real wheels
trapped in rail-bound ricochet
Doomed to retrace the same
Clatter, grind, and bump over
Weary railed corridors of
Trash heap and tent piles
These so called rights of way
The same switchmen, sidings, and schedules
Once incomprehensible to this child of asphalt
Who travelled by power of outstretched thumb
and tattered slab of crayoned cardboard
Except while pulsing through hidden underworld arteries
Buried beneath the movement
That floats, that oily slush and sand
Surface of cities, stormdrained and slick

Insanity of
Entropy is doing the same thing over and over
And expecting a different universe in the end
Creeping osmosis always on my tail
I gotta roll my way till it's time to turn my will molecular
To the replicators, peptide and base pair coded
Repositories of error prone intent

This is my magic hon, just say *spaceball ricochet*
Three times while staring
down a painted white line
Those two lanes and the spirit
That gives us rise
Stiffening belt, sidewall, balance weight
spinning over steamroll kissed blacktop
Don't ever hate on what brought you to life
Or where you've been
Ever

[falling]

One truth is that
Chakras comprise an elevator shaft
That is endless and I am always falling
In dream and in waking
Infinite gravity well
Maximum acceleration
A piece of mythology
Though I strive to achieve
Ideal of that constant
While flailing helplessly
When the world or my thoughts
Push me over

Places within and without me
Are dusklike
And lined with pipes, valves, ductwork
This carapace full of drafts, and spurts of steam
As I breathe or don't breathe
The falling is a given
Whatever flashes by
devoured by nothingness of behind
What looms ahead
Spawn of motion
Children of headrush
Echoing invocation

A throat is but another unending hollow
Among places where word or movement
Give rise to form
The armature of open lips
modulates reality

In unbounded nightfall
Uttered vowels and gasps
Become
Progenitors of phantasm
I do not know if my movement
That fatal attraction of mass
Is part of their reality
But they match my pace, and wrap me
Arms and robes insubstantial
Pointillist incarnation envelopes me
As they begin to whisper
Icicles, flares, rapids rushing into boulders,
Cyclones dauntless,
Their impenetrable sparkle
Infects me
The most tiny speck of void
Devours galaxies of us who are
Primarily wandering desolation

(after Eric Darby's Scratch And Dent Dreams)

I live in a world of ratchet strap dreams...

Where there ain't a store for a good long way
Nor any water
Fit to drink or not
Where what isn't weather worn
Is pack rat chewed
And dried out duct tape
Doesn't hold shit together
But crinkles into tiny
Silver-gray confetti
That clings to my hands like a pain-filled memory
And a gauzy lattice of leftover thread
Laid out in some lesser known system of coordinates
That is useful for absolutely nothing

Where you best pack it all up and take it along
To the Walmart
Or the scrapers will grab it
Though I try to pretend
I don't know why people have such a hankering
For near worthless castoffs

State cop lit me up when one strap,
cheap nylon webbing and bent steel hook
Trailed loose across
Asphalt as I drove by Eloy where the fields smell of cloying mold
And an east wind carries hints of Florence
With its bumper crop of inmates, perpetually over capacity

I lost a good tent, one that I had slept in
And stayed dry all summer
Under the Manzanos' tall pines
Haven to Bear and Deer
But ruthless by late October   when icy rivers of mountain air
Flow down every cut
And over every burnt out swath

In my haste to seek a warmer haven
On a high desert shoreline
Where only fools drive past the hardpack
I mistakenly put my trust in a neon green elastic cord

A tool is anything that can conceivably do a job
Pulled out of a bucket, a shed, a barn
Or as a last resort off a dusty bottom shelf in a small town store
A bent and rusty come-along   a length of galvanized pipe
Knock-off vice grips that bite bloody skin off your finger
But hold on like that chewed up axle nut is Jesus The Savior himself

I slept that night on the sand beneath a cheap blue tarp pitched
With two lengths of pvc water pipe and some prayers
To someone who was not the savior himself
But damn if I didn't sleep well
Once the local partyers had finally had their fill

I live in a world of junkyard dreams
Making not the new and hopeful
from someone elses scratch and dent dreams
But the good enough out of scraps of total wreckage
Or maybe hidden gold that hopefully has not been
Cursed with the seeds of misfortune

And when the law says I have to move off this piece of sand
I'll head down by the border
No metaphor there
Just a warmer spot next to
The remains of an old army camp
Where I can lay my head
And dream one more cast-off dream among the wretched refuse

Without ever a goodnight kiss

Almighty

Present yourself prepared, almighty, for a fight
You've gone on vacation, far too long
Or did you step out for a cigarette, and have no light

Did you wander to the bar? Did you get tight?
They say omnipotent, I guess that means strong
Present yourself prepared, almighty, for a fight

Wise folks hear my callout, brand me not so bright
But humankind is weary, distrustful of your same old song
Or did you step out for a cigarette, and have no light

Were you (a god) assailed by our world? Did you take flight?
Or did you stumble on a kinder sphere, and simply move along?
Present yourself prepared, almighty, for a fight

Did you simply lose yourself? Is your GPS not right?
A pizza and a pitcher? Another game of pong?
Or did you step out for a cigarette, and have no light

Our patience is worn thin. You've fallen from our sight
Abandonment, dereliction, on the face of it seems wrong
Present yourself prepared, almighty, for a fight
Or did you step out for a cigarette, and have no light

Shout! Shout to the tiled rooftops!

that god perhaps might maybe love them
as much as the rolling bins
along the edges of a tree row, a dusty field, or an orchard
where citrus is grown

We come down from ladders among the branches
to taste slices from large bars of halvah, to sip tea
that we may not notice the soreness in our muscles
or our backs

You with you hair in not quite golden rings
wearing a khaki shirt that makes you look too official
but flatters your breasts
you pick up your sack, sling it over your neck
onto your shoulder, prepared for ascension
this gathering in of Earth and Air and Light
before the darkness comes

[Dreams Of]
[Returning]

1.

The precious water of the Jordan
Sprinkled over gardens and concrete walkways
In a place where no stranger could tell with certainty
Where one kibbutz ended and the next began
While walking in the the evenings
Before each night's chill and gunfire set in
Signaling that it was time for those
Who were not on watch to
Sleep for a few hours
Before we rose and returned to the fields

2.

Everyone on both sides of the barbed wire
Already mourned a family member or a friend
In those nights when rifle fire was often exchanged
As a means of saying
We are here, don't try anything
Or as an act of misdirection, that none should anticipate
A particular lethal hour or location

3.
We filled our shoulder sacks with grapefruit
And once we found the ground, emptied them
Into a large wheeled container that was towed by the
Same tractor that had pulled us nodding through
Fields before dawn, as the days were still too hot
To begin our work later
Soon breakfast and tea would arrive
A stainless steel urn and interlocking stacks of tin
containers
Conveyed by a young man from the kitchen
Driving an ancient Susita station wagon

5.
The room I shared with another volunteer
Smelled like dust
And the rat who had died
Who knocked out
The precarious piece of cardboard
That held the unplugged refrigerator's door open
Cutting short both their freedom, and their life

[another american dream]
A Bitter Taste

It's too hot, and the barometric pressure
Is shrapnel and falling
Bodies that tend to remain at rest
A sterilized way of stating that
We.may.rot.where.we.lie
If none remain to mourn
And perhaps the carrion feeders
Deem a place too deeply defiled to return

Adrift in noontime heat and breezes of another desert
I wander empty streets from water's edge
Stone sea walls and cobbled ways of Jaffa
To Disengoff's hollow echoes,
overly bright colors, and concrete sidewalks

I ride shotgun in my friend's Lada
Along the outer fencing of Aza
Well aware that aside from a pocket knife, I am unarmed
I do not know what my friend,
a Russian immigrant, may be carrying

I sit behind the wheel of a rented Fiat
While my cousin, the off duty policeman,
unnecessarily navigates us
Through Palestinian villages
Where people have surely seen better days
He places his semi-automatic pistol
prominently upon the dashboard
Understanding that it is nearly as impossible to
breathe in such gleaming chromium
As it is to casually inhale frangible lead projectiles

Boston Whaler, glistening white slab of glass fibre
Equipped with thrumming diesel engine
A blue-black contrail follows our jounce and shudder
Over Mediterranean roller and chop
To intercept an ancient wooden fishing boat
With far less peeling paint than exposed board
So that all may be turned over and inspected
Among the hand tied nets, the musty tarps
That no lethal things
other than those that have already entered
May come in

Our target practice
The demise of a
Leaking five gallon jug
Perhaps in some mind
A head bobbing above blue-green water
Is a racket designed to chill
The blood of any within earshot
A fitting prelude to our seafood banquet
Overlooking the docks
With many drinks raised, backs slapped
And a few whispered jokes about
My discomfort and ineptitude with firearms

I drift back
Return to my own desert, hungry, dry-lipped
Reaching for water, and
Wishing for a cooler breeze
One that does not burn in my nostrils
Nor cast a bitter taste upon my tongue

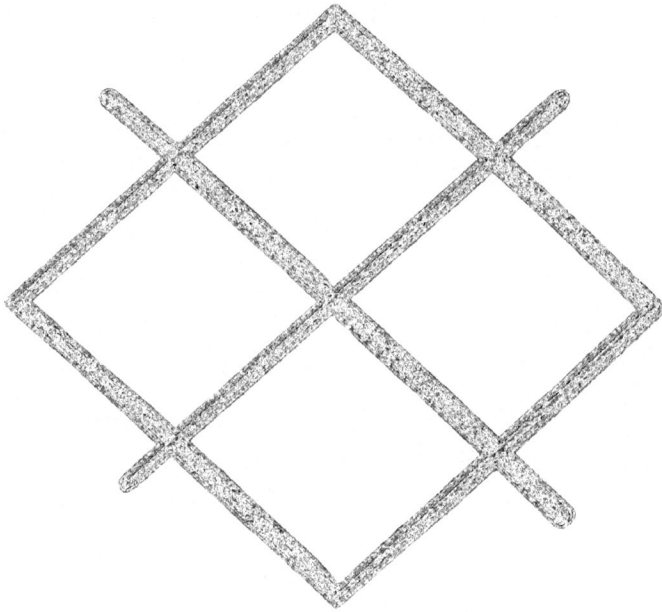

[another american dream]

i believed i knew what my life was about
but i didn't

I tried to hit my marks
remember that any cue in a storm may   save me
from the embodiment of stumble
call me pratfall   call me fool   call me scapegoat
on the line anytime
I appear from my whack-a-mole foxhole   concussed and bled out
like anything starved eventually turns black
the color of desiccated self and exploring angels
cannibalistic symbols of the way I eat death
pick it from my teeth   and thank them for the lesson
the way a labyrinth wends next to itself   moments walk hand in hand
to the heart   a galactic spiral   or a cup of the blackest coffee
we hold that heat within ourselves   adored
in the midst of random bubbles of low entropy
where I am compelled to play like a child again and again   forever   and ever
I am dodging malediction by the power invested in the stubborn and dancing
this is how we minister   this is how we joyride   and damn the sutures
the sacred bloody selves   we carry to each other's arms
maybe this is about home   but maybe it is not
holy wanderer   anointed with ice and pine tar
walks with giant strides   and a voice to chill the hearts of dragons
don't call me earthling   don't call me fool
call me emptiness lost in void
still I continue
I remain

Praise for your collarbones - and the way rope kisses/twisted and silky/
/strands of intertwined trinity flowing/an albatross shadowed armature/
/your breath gives rise and flight/

/hollow we are who take the sky/stuttering or arrowed ascent/
/some domain in which to expand/

/this is the paradox of constriction, snaking of knots/
/are we not some progeny of blessed friction birthed within void/
/unaware of the passing of days and nights/
/perhaps we cheat aeons and furlongs as light and rivers whisper their questions/
/though we are unable to hear/

How you have fallen from heaven,
morning star, son of the dawn!

Did you intend to be menacing
Lucifer, plummeting broken and folded
Perhaps blessed construction of grace and collision
The way impact twists all beings
From on high to the lowly sparkle of those who crawl
Out of holes   Out of a maze of sawgrass and refuse
Out of lifetimes unmeasured

What if time was broken
How would I become aware of the infinite
Step and repeat of your fall or my own
When the leaves turn   and parts of us die
Seemingly of their own accord

There was once a child   or was it a river
Perhaps it was a child born of a mother
Other than an icy headspring
But I cannot recall in this waking that wiped me clean
My mind no more than a sideboard ringed by a thousand
Bowls and glasses

Lucifer,
what might ease you in the place where you may land
Spiraling impact against the unyielding
that is wound to and fro
Within and without all

Perhaps I am merely a waving mouth
Some memory of a tongue and the remains of
Teeth clinging to jawbone and breath
Please tell me who you are and how you came to be
This way...

[I don't believe]
[I'm dreaming]

Fuck you   fuck me   fuck everyone
And everything   fuck timelines and memory
Fuck the way teeth and jaws and ears hurt
Upon waking and throughout the day whenever
The supposedly human entities spread themselves
Upwind of my   miswired neural network
Fuck swelling and the memory of a thousand face punches
And the lesser number of those collisions that took place
Within visible and verifiable ever expanding
Illusion of space   such that mass intrudes upon itself
In ways less than critical   but nevertheless crucial
To a younger person's perception of world and self
Fuck the self and her never met needs
It's lonely at the center of space capsules
Orbiting near ghostS of dogS
Never close enough for insubstantial ear rubs
Never mind a phantom kiss

Fuck the tenuous humanity   this infectious cloak
That dissolves and melds with fascia and fearsome
Page turns of our non-consensual consensus
This is how to breathe they say and
My dissonant nodes scream   don't
Fall for that dreaded element   for
I am naught but never sleeping rust
Remains of hyperactive starstuff
Bombarded with infinite subatomic and macroscopic
Lies, the way it has all been growing
Expansion at some indeterminate rate
Series of dependent variables stretching off
Into bullshit and the scents of biomass
Methane and a whiff of penetrated rectum

I rose from things that were sloughed off and fell away
Never to be much more than just that

[Another American Dream]
[i tried to wave that big dong]
[but she just called me a fake dick]

my name upon everyone else's lips is
artifice pickled in esterified steroids
this is how I assembled myself slowly
molecule by molecule
and when it was time stitch by stitch
while others died drowning in their own analysis

my brain consists primarily of
shredded castoffs of some unknown manufacturing process

Somehow a big generator or a lightning rod was involved
but that was inconsequential
the spark was already in existence between my eyes and legs
as I wandered first cities   then deserts and small towns
where eventually the pick-up lines
my magic incantations
became somewhat more effectual

attempts to remember names   times   and dates are futile
as are my struggles to construct a semblance of life
from the remainder of someone I thoroughly hated

this is how I weave a new reality
from cast-off threads of lost days
and your still warm flesh   a pulsing body
a well-fired furnace   churning out your own heart

[For Comets Who Orbit]
[Formerly Drowning Selves]
[In The Lands Of Asphyxiation]

I feel for traces of some symbiote
Or perhaps the glory of some random goddess or god
Having entered me
The way my abdomen heaved in twilight and the hollow below
My sternum crawled and fell into
Seeming emptyness while I rode all this as gently as possible
How do I keep up   on the back of a bucking spirit
Dig in but don't dampen this perfect
Excruciating ride any   more than I must
Hold the reins   like lost love
Or a desert valley sunrise
After long cold night
My eyes having followed Orion
To one or another dreams of freedom
This valley   This valley   This valley
And the wind that sculpts the surrounding hills
So they all look to be leaning toward the east
Do they know   the distant ocean that once
Covered them   Hid them   Held them deep
Still exists   relentless thrashing of waves
Rhythm of tides within all of us   earthbound
The glassy stillness of a shallow bay
Disturbed only by the prow of a passing lobster boat

don't care that it's midnight
cause anyone who fucks with me
be fucking with someone who feels she has damn little to lose

There's a way that blade nestles into fabric of my pocket
Like it wants to believe in my flesh's myth, some long lost epic
Regarding my cuddlesome nature
Likely mistranslated from the original Hebrew or Greek because
Empires always work that way, hamstrung by frayed wire
A broken sandal
A scribe's shaking hand
But that knife, the way it snaps open
Like every damn atom and molecule
Ever moving among this ever expanding
Ever baffling mess
Envies the miracle of   beveled edge
Applied along this sweep of recurved steel
Like maybe I have no other purpose
But to wear this blade
Like it's the only one I could ever marry
Or at least carry to my bed   most every night
Because neither one of us adheres to convention
Clinging only to blood and survival
At least until the darkest new moon
When some overall-clad bozo
Or some venom-spitting hit woman
Calls me out

Ca-Cha!
  or
[Another American Dream Dies Here]

They teach you to never draw from the drop but I'm skeptical
When staring down the opening of a muzzle
And her expression spelled death
So I let my pocket sand fly toward her eyes
As I mouthed his name, Gribble
Hoping I'd bought a moment to dodge

Should not have come to this, I should have booked out of Dodge
I'd only needed to pee, but America is skeptical
Of girls like me, and much less kind than Gribble
I growled like I needed a muzzle
And did not meet her eyes
Donut holes of death

In her hands, double stack, friable projectiles o'death
What could I offer thee,
to be standing on the corner of Grant & Dodge
Hands in pockets, Tucson headlights blinding my eyes
I may yet survive but I am skeptical
Under influence of malice and muzzle
My vain attempt to channel Gribble

Chlordane and pyrethrins will not make you sick,
until they do, so sayeth Gribble
His fall from bugbane to deskbound hatchet man,
dealer of corporate death
But now at every turn, sprouting stands of magazine and muzzle
In gun metal nation, it has always been this way for many,
how does a body dodge
And not fall skeptical
In face of new moon legions of manchildren with hooded eyes

Should I tear out my eyes
Perhaps in vain attempt
to close some cosmic chasm between self and Gribble
Or am I in vision of stall door, grout lines, and bleedout, skeptical
May I become destroyer of her hope to deal death
Mystical channel of evasion, dodge
Spawn of black powder, and her erect muzzle

You are invited to witness wedding of flesh and fragment,
officiated by muzzle
This is how trans people die under gaze of hate brimmed eyes
Misdirection of pocket sand and dodge
My failure to become empty container of infinite Gribble
Imperfection at headwaters of human,
summons none but servants of death
While of freedom, america remains skeptical

They say to never dodge from the drop,
line of fire, gaping muzzle
But spectral eyes peel stubborn layers of stickers and paint,
signifiers of skeptical
Farewell, Dear Gribble,
from this land where difference leads to death

[THIS IS NOT A DREAM]
[IN THE MIDST OF]
[FISSURE]

How do I tune myself to the key of human
All stripped gear and joint crack
Borrowed cup of protons, ersatz embodiment
Speaker echoes pop refrain of
Radioactive! Radioactive!
While self-proclaimed holy people raise their hand
Avert their gaze

The way an imported strongarm cop
Gets up in my face
Rides my ass round a small town
Brands me outside troublemaker
Like BLM and Antifa coming down your deadend dirt track
For your chicken coops, broke down trucks
Folding chair churches, your heroin family legacies

This is how I poison every planet and person with
Dim Mak and virus, contagion of woman-loving faggotry
When it seemed that every adopter of alternate spellings
Wound their spells
In the end to taint and gatekeep

This is how I walk away from battle
Show you my spine of trinitite and blinding flash
Show you my ass, godzilla-toppled granite, folly of humon
Scream bug-eyed at purposeful grimace of non-fistable
Cunt and swagger

This is not a chokeout or a submission
Just a nod and hallmark you can slide into a hot hip pocket
At the corner of fever dream and soaked sheets
Maybe you need a new goddess
Or a scratch and dent tuning fork
To help you sing your song
Frequency of yowl, toothmark, and thrash
We are all born of vibration and longing
Baptized in void

This is how to wade through one thousand leagues of self
Simply to grasp my hand

[Propagating The Cuttings Of]
[Another American Dream]

Nothing good can ever come of this
Life in concrete bunkers
The way mole people descend from on high
Guided only by scents of death and decomposition
This is a path that wends inevitable to
Nothing good can ever come of this
The way our feet and our bodies marched through Ramallah
Below the caftan-covered men
Standing on their balconies, bearded
Dressed in their scornful and sad expressions
What does one do in the face of coercion
Unleashed in the aftermath of war

We were blue-shirted, wearing white hats to match some flag
There is always some flag waving where
Nothing good can ever come of this
Where the unwanted, the undesirable are used
As a weapon against the unwanted, the undesirable
Any tactic to keep another wave of us
From breaking upon their shores
From further contaminating their great cities
That were never emerald, nor lined with a single fleck of gold
But surely radiated that illusion, the beneficence of empire
Standing to salute those flags forever, and ever, amen
Always in some place where
Nothing good can ever come of this

And they will lead you to become your own infinitesimal empire
The sun always sets on those who are turned to fight
Over grains of bloodstained sand

Remember always that the big three or four or five
Stole from us all   our vines and fig trees
They feed upon desperation and the will to survive
Then inject a venom that transforms their minions
Into their own image

[In My American Dream]
[All I See Are Dead Children]
[But All I Write About Is Bullshit]

A never ending trailer of
schools, war zones, famine
flashes across
my mind's
silver-toned living room screen
Cinerama, IMAX, Dolby brain
Yes, it surrounds
while I write about
a fifty-four year old TV show
and my father's bloodless death
on a Serta
perfect
sleeper

Fun is fun
and grief is
backing track
before
stop-action bang up
memories molotov
the corners of my mind

When the cafe was cordoned
For ZAKA to scrape up
bits of splattered flesh
that all may be returned
as complete as possible
but a rocket was dispatched
to collapse an apartment block
full of families
in Gaza
a sacred office was blatantly defiled
again

I walked Jerusalem streets
suspect
out of place
unarmed but alive

Where's Waldo in camo
stalks an american school room
All bravado suspended
what would I do

Everyone asks
how much
can a ten-year-old bleed
I need to know
what if she and her best friend
were eviscerated by the same bullet
Is that one or two
thoughts and prayers

I write about spiders
and long-dead friends
while fresh graves are dug
I recall the feel of the shovel
the heft and smoothness
worn wood against bare hands
as I dropped rocky earth
on to the cover of my mother's casket
The lasered gazes of many assembled
did not erupt exit wounds and geysers
but that was the last week
that I ever wore a dress

I watch brightly animated high school students
demolish a mountain of monjayaki
over feelings evoked by a kiss
I contemplate that I have never gone seriously hungry
for food

I am buried by an
avalanche of
black and white
UHF TV images
Manipulated
Missionary visions
of distended bellies

Sponsor a good book, a bowl of millet
and baptism
with a proper christian name
It was already too late
for little Joseph
when we found him

In the city of ACAB
(that is) spelled
with a U
nineteen small ghosts
process silently
around
the station
They need no spies
They will blow no horns
Their lack of faith
will topple those walls

Reiteration

Stone bridges always lead me to Oświęcim
A river drifts through the camps
into the old city
Green farmer's fields in summer
Wind whipped roils
of choking coal smoke
in December
when heavy air weds
the darkest of icy roads
Phantom sun, a moving disk
to mark day's time
withholds a finger's brush of warmth
to thaw the skin of now grown children
Their parents' feigned blindness
mirrored in concrete smiles
displayed to the perpetual procession

[A Different Dream]
[your average creature of the shadows]
[nursing a long-broken heart]
[and a rebellious meat suit]
[awaits resuscitation]

In a remote corner of the beautiful toxic wastelands
where we come and go as comets
wanderers quickly fading from memory
against a backdrop of every day's needs
each reeling from sucker punch perpetual assault
myself an unrecognizable landscape
perhaps some twisted likeness of survivor

This is how I know
I don't know
Don't know
I don't
Don't

This is how I reel
Under influence of imposed vertigo
Endeavoring to not drop belay
Because there may still be someone
A precious body, limbs, and mouth
At the other end
The way we are harnessed
Together for life support, awaiting resuscitation
I don't believe in reincarnation
So we better make this good

Every day I talk to a ghost
(for Doug Smode - written summer 2023)

It's not like we were close
But I wonder if I could have gifted you
A moment's peace, when you needed it
You joyful man-dragon, careening across floors and forests
Calling out *motherfucker motherfucker*
Like pain plus will plus that word
Burst open infinite reservoirs
Pulling, that big black bus
By two hooks pierced through your butt cheeks
While I just whimper *shit* every time I accidentally
Attempt to shatter shin on trailer hitch

Perhaps you were the stealth Badass of Sad
Concealed saboteur, mindfuck spread wide open to infinity
Intertwined with twisted jute while
Spirits oozed out your every pore
Swallowed you whole
The times they did

This is how some unicorn riders fall
Like earthshatter, cloudbreak, & legend
While others skip off our atmosphere but are also
Lost to us who starve for shimmer and war cry

Northern lights never had the key
or anything to say about much of anything
Except everything

Sometimes it's nice to have a near stranger
among the ghosts I loved who detest me
But still persist
So I talk with you in ordinary ways
On desert monsoon nights
After days of heat stroking me
To death tease, oblivion, and convulsion

When that moon plays hide and seek
When footfall flushes quail
Stumbling into camp wheezing
Leg spent and chest tight
This is how we count stars
When the sky suddenly clears
Like they've always been our treasure

(whatever holds me)
(to these places)

Feelings are gravel
Indigestible life that
Blankets gravitational
Undertow you are distant
But everpresent echo in
Wind blown telegraph
Sad that the speed of light
Is often times too slow
An impediment to immediacy
Of fusing starstuff   your periodic
Proud orbit was created for longing
And collision with whatever remains
Within this blooming, my expanse of
Phosphor and oil field grime
Where I am forever seeking Dallas
Or perhaps some other city where we were
Bound shockwave and steel
This is how endless afterburner births
Memory and interstate
This is how banshees
Cannot help but stop and smile
Whenever we come home

[The American Dream Of]
[Smasher / Devourer]
[Lays Down By The Riverside]

The old shell feels like armor
But is only a leather jacket
That some fucker tried to rip off my back
In the pit, before I put an elbow to his jaw
In hope of some relocation of his body or
His brain, before I had to bluff or sneak my way
Past the rutted and puddled lot to hopefully free concrete

Should I cradle an empty bottle like some holy child wrapped
In tanned and dyed cowhide
Like any makeshift weapon may climb the heavens
To become savior within cradle of my fingers

How does a person learn to worship something
When grace itself is only a means to reach blessed escape
And stained glass only serves to bend and conceal the sun
Such a foreign concept when fevered Saturday nights and
the butts of a thousand
Chain-smoked cigarettes lay scattered under Sunday's dawn

Hazy-brained,
boots weaving that heaving asphalt over by the tracks
In some still blue-lawed town
where soon the plaid and pleated be singing
Down By The Riverside, and
I've found no rest from my heavy load

4:55AM Transmission

Purgatory mind rises at
Fuck 4:55AM
Sunday morning
Is that
what the phone screen says

Broke down on
corner of Penance
and Wheelspin
Billows of smoke
Zero to peace
in infinity

Pull back into second
tryin' a grab blacktop
But motionless
when I come to
and wonder
what I truly deserve

Joy Division is droning
Transmission in my brain
Behind piercing high tinnitus walls
I pack laser audio weaponry
sights trained on shattered neurons
They jangle broken

Radio...

Inside I sport tinsel
stolen from dumpsters and sidewalks
of forgotten holidays
Broken ornaments hang
no more than shards
on loops of monofilament
No hooks to catch a thought
on cast-off chunks of crumbling concrete

Listen...

Corroded rebar
never rings true,
not when I strike it
with bare flesh or thought
The stain of oxide, acrid
A souring world I wander in my hollows

...living in the night
...waiting

I learned to keep moving
keep walking
keep distance to survive

...as though nothing was wrong

Back streets, and tunnels
Anywhere
I could stretch my legs
Practice the Illusion
of walking strong

Staying...just staying out...

I feared their power as much as my own

Dance...radio...

Wireless thought injection
Flailing limbs
Swim upstream
Aquatic ladder
Does it rise to some mythic home

Dance...radio...

Breath of panic
And bedsweat
I can caress this ceiling
With sun's rise looming
Just cross the line

...no longer enough

What do I know
when I crack open a bone
What tune will it sing to me
when a body's learnt wrong
Marginal notation
That course correction will
not unwander a stray

No language...
...the show

 I feared their power as much as my own

And we could dance...

[Another American Dream]
[Return Road From A Suscon]

We been living most of our lives
By dying glow of dashboard light
Fading yellow, roadside hell
Ditch or truck stop
I was driving till I nearly drop
The visions and the voices calling me
Out
Like I don't need this world no more
Like some dirt casino parking lot
Stumbling players sporting bolo ties and plastic cups
Like their threats and jacked pickup trucks
Somehow make them more real
Than you or me or the bruises we've inflicted
Fading into dawn following dawn
Thousands of miles of suffering asphalt apart
Magic of the road is that it seems to rise to my command
And I pretend it doesn't own me even if it knows me
Some mountain side dirt track
Switchback, washboard against which I've thrown my body
And the wheels thereof uncounted times
I'm the Sisyphus of the driver's seat, sagging
Flagging spirit of the path to the same door
I just just drop to my knees
Fall on my side
And hit rewind

[I Dream My Way]
[Across America's]
[Four Lane Blacktop]

We are tires skimming braille. Five thousand pound
phonograph needle scraping up the billion names of God
inscribed in hot-patch lines and curls. Floating upon curses,
invective spewed toward universe and humankind. The road
is layered with love letters in Sanskrit, Khmer, Greek. A
random Hebrew or English exclamation stretches across half
the four lane where twin tracks of new oil give way to older
patchwork hand laid by sun-crazed workers.

Beyond where Second Street turns back to highway, begins a
skyward grind, yucca and brown grasses give the land to pine
and grazing pasture. Horses don't give a damn. They ignore
the coming and going of pickup trucks, clunker cars, the
random motorhome hop-scotching small town speed zones
and stoplights.

My arms guide the tin can, gutted to nakedness, echo chamber
for spinning and reciprocating metal chunks, wind noise,
a-capella of blacktop and concrete amplified in this rolling
drum supported by hollow stays. My superstructure surfs
harmonic as arms guide front tires. Two patches of rubber
massage asphalt, pull us around off-cambered sweepers,
curves that seem designed to throw lone fools like me off the
side of mountains.

I already have no feeling in my feet.

My tin can is smooth where the road is smooth, and willfully unforgiving everywhere else. On the trip out, we almost lost it on an exit sweeper, oddly tilted concrete slabs pounded askew and deeply scarred by countless tides of big rigs seeking fuel and black coffee. We jumped, crashed porpoise-like, when I tried to gentle on the brake. I whipped round, rag doll random urban cowgrrrl, with maybe one too many notches in my belt, strapped in for the ride. A quick prayer, or was it a curse, escaped my lips as the suspension made a horrible racket. Thank Goodness, nothing broke.

Today I raced, up at dawn. Fifteen miles to town from that dry camp near the bottomless lakes where I'd waited for yet one more doctor who could not cure me but maybe could help. I burnt in the shade for a week, rays bouncing under corrugated covering, attempting to recharge, too weak to leave.

They call it a ramada but it had no sides, this place where I threw my cot, and sweat till shadow shrank away, drove me into my rolling cave. A thin coating of white paint covers the stamped metal interior. I clung to a once frozen water bottle, quickly melting in this tiny world, bound together by spot welds and beads of sealer.

Lay me down on stove top, lay me down in toaster oven, lay me down by river heat-stroke. Sing me delirium songs. I am penny on your grave, not enough, not enough. I would be more. A silver coin, a gift to pay your way while I remain.

I raced away from that place. Through the cow town where the side streets reminded me of Asheville North Carolina, quiet and tree-lined. I arrowed down Second Street on a mission. Gas, water, ice, air, check crankcase, and go. Roll out miles before the heat slaps me down, before fatigue makes me more stupid, before music, bells and voices rise behind constant ringing in my ears, before I hear the chorus of my name being called in time with my tremors.

My arms guide my hands. Caress the wheel. Conn this too-tall vessel of sheet metal and waking dreams up toward Mescalero, climbing through edge of cloudburst.

I stop at the top before the descent takes me by deserted gas stations, the tribal community center, and a church that appears to be suspended mid-air on misty days. The air is clear here in the minutes between bursts of traffic, troughs between waves of eighteen wheelers that shake my little van. Diesel fumes choke me, fog my brain if I take off my mask. The thin layer of carbon is inadequate protection against a world that seems determined to torture me, to cast me out. Trouble is there is almost nowhere left to run.

In a quiet moment, I slip off my mask for a quick drink. The scent of pine slaps me hard even as cool, damp air refreshes my skin. My ears ring more loudly, and I can feel swelling grow in my face and neck. Best to get my mask on quick. Best to head down, back to the low desert.

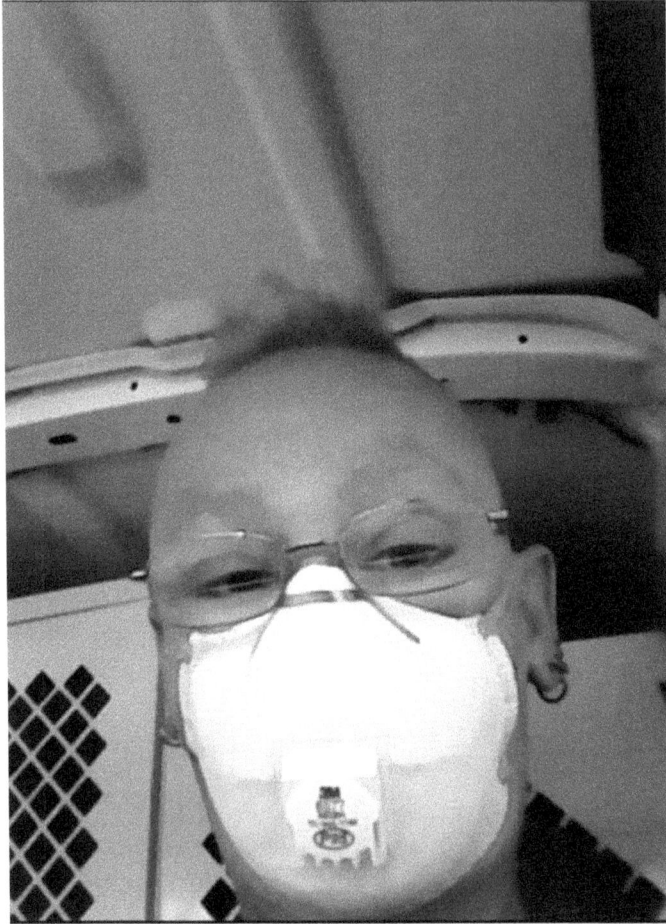

A Priest, a Minister, and a Rabbit walk through my dream
And I praise the Fluffy Bunny for being most wise

Life changes
The way I plummet down a well shaft
or from a suspension bridge
to kiss the elasticity, ceaseless flow of river

Everything rolls downhill
in a world of gyroscopes and blood
I force myself to eat because I am balanced
astride my fence
having witnessed so many wastings away

Circumstances change
Health changes
Capabilities change
People change
Communities change
The durability of magic comes into question

Perpetual dance, is it energy and mass
that we need to interrogate
or the impression that we are all either villain or saint
If you cut me open you would only find
a city and a sewer, not much different than many others
born into this bubble of nearly infinite improbability

[In Last Night's American Dream]
[Everyone Was Famous For Three Minutes]
[On The Internet] [But Not Me]

No drama
No affair
With a punk-pop influencer

I didn't die hiking the grand canyon
My remains found ravaged by a solitary mountain lion
A funeral party of turkey vultures
Turned lazy loop-the-loops
Rode a massive thermal
While waiting for sloppy seconds
GoPro still strapped over my backward ball cap
Captured their flight for insta-posterity

I was never finger fucked by a touring comic
With more than one hundred thousand followers
On a nondescript bed in some nondescript hotel room
Following a pleasant dinner in dubuque or albuquerque

The skin on my face hangs far too loosely
Social currency of career, home, health   all fell away
Like the hair that was once upon my head

My life is filled with sex tips for the highly allergic person
Trapped in a party full of heavily perfumed bodies
Room permeated with icy demeanor of the young and phobic

I am lost among legions of people who are seen as nobodies
Who would rather unalive than be me

Each generation believes they invented voluntary
Discorporation
Suicide
While having never gathered sufficient magic
To face the final boss

Those who do not see themselves as future artifact
Are doomed to repeat themselves ad infinitum
Tethered to whack-a-mole cams and cranks
With never a hammer in sight

We rise and fall
On swell and trough
Exhausted from performing
The dog paddle of survival

You got soda and drugs
Nootropics and makeup tips
Lips unchapped for your audition

It's always a good run till
It ends on the floor
Supine
Unconscious
All the assembled stepping over
A familiar curiosity
Perhaps a wise or kind human
Would turn you on to your side
But they don't

It ends piled against a brick wall
In a clapped-out toyota
With bad brakes, squeaky steering,
and its own internal debris field

It ends with the flickering of lights,
and the same stupid song again
The way we swim into void of summer's heat still rising
In some two-bit town

It ends when I shut off the smartphone
And roll into panic
That stalks me on the borders
Of oblivion

[In The Middle Of The Dream]
[Everything I Once Craved]
[Makes Me Retch]

A body can only withstand so much nasty
Before it declares itself too ancient
For indulgences we so long considered tasty
Spices too scalding, spine twisting backbeats
Dark sky marathons, nights racing sunbreak
Now thoughts of death take center stage, fill my screen

Now Death, you fill my screen, hog the stage
Can't breathe in this haze, antihistamine and nasty
I long for sweet unconscious sunbreak
Or epiphany, some gift from progenitors, ancient
Perhaps a sweet caress, comfort in relentless backbeat
Has my life gone flat, that errant tasty

Dragging a deadpool for that errant tasty,
  in my life gone flat
Steal that spotlight,
  take the stage on my horizon's pixelated scream
Modulate the grim, you reaper of backbeat
Don't run away, don't do me nasty
Don't leave me alone, ancient
Lost in dark sky, racing sunbreak

That's my sunbreak race, hiding in dark sky
A desert isn't flat, and dust isn't tasty
But it is the flavor of my skin, ancient
Perhaps a sensation on your palate
   when I occupy a small box on your screen
   or stumble on to a stage
Not so much nasty
But the way a river moves, ventricular backbeat

Ventricular backbeat, this is the way of rivers
And sky, rhythm of sunbreak
But slow grind nasty
Genus and species of tasty that never falls flat
On stage or palm top screen
For I who have arrowed cross sky, from daybreak to ancient

Dogged by ancient bullshit and heartbreak
Pulsating backbeat of conscience, on banks of Eden's river
Every memory a demon set upon a palmtop stage
Where sunbreak cues a waxen sky
Steamrolled in midst of infinite tasty
Ever nasty, forever nasty

Small screen, portal to heartbreak both current and ancient
Beeping nasty beat
   should be tossed in a river or into Mount Doom
Heartbreak and daybreak are the same to the haunted,
   so it is I've lost my taste

[Another Dream Of]
[Taking On That Sheen]

I tried to turn my self into steel
stainless   solid   impermeable
a polished surface to reflect any gaze
vaporize curious retinas
cool   look up at the sky
it's falling again
watch it play over and across my skin
like second hands
and the moon's pull on the water that you are

instead I transformed into quicksilver
a self impossible to contain in any safe way
take a teaspoon or a touch of me
upon your finger and taste death
the surety of dissolution
this self that I am cannot
be uploaded because I never retain
the same shape long enough
columns of liquid ones and zeros
coalesce for a fraction of a moment
but continuously rearrange themselves

there is no way to detect the errors within my being
no opportunity to correct something
that changes so quickly
it may not even exist

[Another American Dream]
[Some Stillborn Convocation]

I could be my Mata Hari
Betrayer of self to self
Or a pop up advertisement
For the free iPhone
Perpetually un reachable
I am already well versed
In incompetence and rhyme
Janky ass 'merican poets
Cling to thought crime
Aged out and sucked dry
This is not how to trickle joy
Into starving mouths
Of barbed wire and topple
How can flesh negotiate
Exothermic hailstorms
And ill winds that gather
None but
The wearing away of
Even our most calcified remains

Strike up the band, boys
Gather round for our new image
Of artificial thought and shadowbox
We see an end to your dreams
For we have become
Network vampires, centralized orchestrators
Of distributed bland, push tech of major triad
Living dead poets
The way that business suits and street hustlers
Perform transient bonds
Electron transfer, is that a particle in your pocket
Polly Purebred, or do you breathe molten lilac
Scent of sanitation and restraint that makes me gag
Like you got crossed wiring, beta code
Contagion of bit rot and unlubricated latex

Who stands behind this joyless contraption
Dislocated jumble
Of ball joints who gathers rejection
In ways that others grab up manna and gold coins

Rig me up to some hanging tree
You're going to see that illusion
Of me shaking free
(But when a body)
(But when a body)
But when a body is nearly at rest
My convocation of hopeless and stubborn
Sits under a sun
That shares no warmth

Divination

While suture flows through my skin
Interrupted by knot
The twining and pull of forceps and gloved hand
Where I had torn once again
At juncture of Gilson's device
And my stubborn desire
That always seems to exceed
The strength of my flesh

I receive your word
Unexpectedly upon this cold table
Where I feel whatever may seem to be self
Slipping away
And not when I had walked the path
To that descending stair
While I was tethered offering
While rigging and song
Held no meaning
Beyond that they were present
And had not failed me

You tell me that my trials
Will multiply far beyond
What can be imagined

And how can I imagine more
After I have been
So sorely tested
Over countless vitality sapping
Turns of season
When I'd finally
Come to believe
That I had
Learned to take a punch

How can I find some
Path forward
Amidst my own torrents
Such that I
Or those who remain
In whatever aftermath awaits
May dare assign meaning
To my deathwalk

After Life Suspended

Help me if you can
to not run the light
to not nod off
There's a cop
corner of Pecos and Arizona Ave at 3:39AM
Turn left
to float south on a ribbon
created by my motion
through fields sprayed damp in circles
Pungent with green and fusarium
I breathe my way
to Casa Grande
supercenter tarmac

There my runes
Intent and devotion
writ that day in pen and gentian violet
frighten off a rag-tag vanload of sober evangelists
My chosen form of space clearing
display forearms and fists
against tide of holy rolling squadron
Smile as they drive off heads shaking
semaphore of their
shared sense of certainty

Hook holes are oozing
all down my body's front
I choose my stigmata
My miracles performed by mortal hands
Sometimes this is how we spell family
in a different birthing ward

My old steroid-weakened collagen hide
never strong enough
to fight Earth's clutches for long
"Gravity pulls my face
pulls my skin"
A bit of suture
stitches together my
nothing but memories

You all flew like angels
triumphantly wounded
My pride in everyone else
while everlong questioning myself

I am checked and weather-worn driftwood
unrecognized remains
rolling on shoreline of shut-eye
still hearing music's echos
There are places in me
born to reverberate

Vision of rig lines
glint of chain links and eyebolts
captured in crisscross of spotlights above
before I turned to blindfold
Turned in and outward
Turned on a swivel
Turned into offering

Shut-eye shut-eye shut-eye
and drift a bit
on the edge of recall
That searing returns
as I slowly spin
before daystar's hammer slaps my van
roasts me into parched waking
Consecrated broiler where I nightly toss and turn
Dream
Now

I lost my faith on the day I met you
Sliding between rows of folding wooden chairs
I mean   who wears a white dress to a small town
Cockfight   a muddy backyard   strewn with refuse
The remains of cheroots   and   cracked red plastic cups
You Fallen Madonna
You Percocet Queen
Dreamland smile and a deft touch
This is how a knife's edge   seeks
Very much noticed   along my paralyzed
Diaphragm   I am forever fortunate
Lucky that I understand
That breathing is optional
But venom is necessary to sustenance
My construction of sublimated toxins
And cast off bits of gravel
Who can now only wield a pen following the intoxication
Of sleep and hopeless mornings   while birds endlessly claw
And peck
At seams in the roof

[After Helicopter Helicopter's song *Please Please Tito*]

[Poem by a kid who]
[has been called **[Christ Killer]** one too many times]

Incarnatus

I'll kill your savior
To save this world of clay
To bring judgment day, I'll do you that favor

I will save you the work, take on the task,
wrapped in plastic label, I'm the new scapegoat flavor
You('re) turned out in gold trimmed vestments,
power always struts that way, you make it pay
I'll kill your savior

I don't need no waiver, for my murderous behavior
Already seen the interrogator, this is what I call foreplay
To bring judgment day, I'll do you that favor

Your double standard, blatant religion-couched misbehavior
Sowing hate and greed, violence every day, as is your way
I'll kill your savior

I'll eat the world's disfavor, it's a well familiar flavor,
I'll take on that labor
I'll bounce my way through every day, singing na na na hey hey
To bring judgment day, I'll do you that favor

No need to help me
I won't waver
Like I said, I'll kill your savior
To bring on judgment day, I'll do you that favor

[This Is]
[Replica]

Dear people, dear humzans, and buttercups

Dear buttercream dreams, V-twin riders, wheelwrights
and still born wraiths filled with stillborn wrath

Dear others, mumzers, replicas, and replicants

This is one used-up old shit's goodbye
This is how storybook endings will slam us
Butterfly and dead flowers sandwiched between
Crackling incoherent pages, some supposedly revered poet's
Delusional stream of wine soaked demi-conscious precious
Bullshit and self-professed post-nut clarity

But I digress

This is a letter from a lost child left unfound
This is a reminder that compass needles
Can only spin and deceive in poleless spheres
This is a world written in crayola and soft jumbo pencil
Upon the interior of a yellowing skull
Scrawled in marker across gray expanses
Of doorless metal stalls
This is how you can lead a horse to water
But you sure can't browbeat or otherwise coerce
A frozen four year old, five year old, adolescent
Nor your ancient evil auntie, not slab-bound but the epitome
Of granite, and the ice that comes and goes like
Only wanderers and seasons bother to drop a word
Or mutter some tattered scrap of song or rhyme

But I digress

Often times the concept that there are lifeboats or lifelines
Is nothing more than that, in lives left on the drawing board

I once bought a drafting table, surplus deemed obsolete
But in my dreams of myself there is no market
For us who have long borne the marks of exile
And secrets burned into our substance

Jam one more penny in this fuse box and pretend
That trails of carbon,
and the scent of singed phenolic are healing
Or perhaps replace me with something ceramic
Because icons brushstroked with the colors of your longing
Give more comfort than your failed necromancy

But I possibly digress

I never had the power to blot out death or infidelity
Never found the means to resurrect my self
I was never so much an irresistible object
As their compulsions were, to themselves irresistible
So I spun myself into razor wire and ether

I never unearthed the mystery of dim mak
Because the death touch is everyone else's
Compulsions to suck off a bit of my being
While they name me stunted and insufficient

Beauty Regimen

Sweat and soap and water
Too much sun
Stand or sit in moonlight with
Bucket and brush

Too much sun
Dust and wind
Bucket and brush
Blue washcloth

Dust and wind
Makes years of days
Blue washcloth
Over my skin

Make years of days
Recline in moonlight
In good land called badlands
Always bring water

Practicing Sums

The Holy Water
and Blue
equals
the knots she tied
gently between pearls
plus the rise of foot's ball
on the And
between
One, Two

Like when life
hinges on atria
But poets speak of
ventricles,
concrete,
glazed bricks
of subway walls

Forged rails
impose balance
on movements, momentum (forces)
Total Blue retained

Energetic knots
gently move
her fingertips
to tie

They taught us
to begin
counting at one
Summing, plus one
plus one, plus one

Drops from Holy Faucets
play in
double cut time

One And, One And,
One And, Blue
equals the hinges of life
which concrete poets
try to force
into ventricle and song

Involuntary Prophets
never know
to say, yes
They stand
atrial chamber
forged knot
to forces
Always imprisoned
between summoning
voices

[More News from the Underworld]

I am not the being who writes the words in this journal. She is a woman who glides through mornings wearing a long black dress and my bones. Her midnight hair is better than mine has ever been since it was first cut, since school transformed me in most apparent aspects, into something brittle, an awkward representation of young human who lined the wrong wall of basement classrooms, enveloped in the futile striving to tie her shoes with proper bow or some year to learn to interpret symbols, signals arrayed on a printed page, books of mundane adventures of children who consistently conformed to expectations of church and state. Those were not written by a woman who glides through mornings wearing a long black dress and my bones. Her midnight hair far better than mine has ever been

My brittleness in some aspects laid hidden, buried beneath a growing roundness that never in those days wore a black dress but spent mornings in a basement among tunnels lined with yellow and black metal signs

Later there were open infinite stairways, precipice in a kingdom of glass and air, above seas of shining tile. How does a child learn to be a superhero or warrior in such a place. My legs refused to conform, to commit motions of ascension and descension, while the only folklore passed down were mundane adventures of children who consistently conformed to expectations of church and state. Oh, yes... and their faithful family dog, long deceased, destined never to bark at the margins of this apocalypse, at whatever stalks my nights, nor the woman who glides through my mornings, and is writing this

Deadnamed before deadnames, twist of enteric rememberance, long before the years of rockstar necrophilic love, I was the dead. Walking unacknowledged except in service of the crowbars of synagogue and state, the all normative omnipotent conformity of survivors and displaced goaded by echoes, voices of the missing and the murdered

Fuck you and your self-fulfilling prophecies surrounded by your agents, church going educators, thoroughly brainwashed five year olds spewing hardsell of consistent conformity. My impossibility, for which meaningful symbols, signal arrays, had not yet been crafted. But all difference needed to be trampled for its own salvation, and the comfort of others. All must be shielded from my apparent inferiority, a debt only partially paid in acquired brittleness. I was inadequately concealed and closeted despite superheroic effort

[Recycled American Dream]
[Self Sabotage] [Is] [My Birthright]

I can't remember the touch of your hand
But I still remember your voice
A repeating end   a chorus   the way chainlinks
Are locked   a procession of yous   by so many other names
All sound the same   because I fall in love forever vocal
That auditory burn   my ears high   on what
While you are tripping   speaking of molecules
And orbit   next to me in my Fiat   an accidental
Party to a gas line   the way I rationed myself to you
Never finding my own   naked body palatable
In our unlikely   In our non-event
Fear and the damnation   of that self and all assembled
How do I fuck up my life over and over
Let me recount the ways

[Dreaming Of]
[The Small]

The world is constructed of tiny particles
Imbued with near immeasurable power
Embodiment of ceaseless movement
and infinite pain
The way a sliver of glass slides sidewise
Penetratrates sole of foot, and awareness
The way an aggregate, named lover
Ceases, emulates the appearance of frozen
Is over, when nothing ever ends
In the sense of   images we cling to
Ripples and collision, on pond and
In an eyeball scanning felted table

It all comes down to splash, clack, and chatter
We mimic seabirds and battery hens
In time .we.too. will neglect to preen
Our strut lost in sands and infinite smallness
Of divinity
Perhaps I have become ancient
Silently destroyed by this world
Or otherwise vanishingly small

[American Dreams of]
[Meat Ghost, Most to Toast]

Am I scaring all the people
with weapon of myself
Ammunition snaps
girl, I'm just a meat ghost
for your derision

Not like I rate some love
like vampire or non-CHUD
The flip cards of fashion
buried me in dust

Youth culture mantra
gone bust
Hey hey it's
old people smell
replacing crust
Hey hey it's
notification, action required
Pass the sniff test, you must

High caloric, carbohydrate
in break neck sweetness
and orange men they do trust
Doors they bust
Militarized
with their guns and ammunition

Kill them in beds, sleeping
or simply getting off their lust

One nation
under green backed delusion
of policy played off as confusion
while we biohack and scratch
for some cover and safe calories

Dream of leaving
a bit better behind
Pushing hands
Years that formed us
Buried corridors lined
with thought crime
Or maybe games of less game
are still games
when we fall for them

[Another American Dream of]
[Rebranding]

CoreCivic
Formerly
Corrections Corporation Of America
Formerly
The Plantation
Formerly
Every shackle and lash applied to an unwilling body
In pursuit of one's own comfort, profit, and position
In the volumes that were
written in an alphabet of manifest
Destiny of God's chosen   who seek to monopolize
Word, wealth, muzzle blast, airwave
Legacy of fear and force   is not a legacy nor lineage
Yet it is lauded   as such
In far too many war rooms
Disguised as sunday pulpits

Child

Child of bleach bottle, child of sharps container
nourished by the only three foods you can eat

Child of psoriasis and wheeze, rattle of nebulizer
chuff from a green plastic tube housing a tiny pressure vessel
alloy, wrapped in cautions, colors of your nation's flag

Child of particulates, daddy's powerstroke superduty
sauron's doomcloud
an icy finger traces course of bone and cartilage
duet of spinous process and decay
worship of hubris and stubbornness
in service of destruction and barest survival

What would it mean to thrive
and who would fund such an experiment
What metric does one apply to lives lived in dreamstates
unbearable pressure-cooker of consciousness
is every morning's jammed release valve
calendars measured in explosions
splatter of seconds, shrapnel of minutes
How does one record that on a timecard
chore list, a medication schedule
A hundred million dinners that must be on time
How do you sometimes dodge backhands
autofire belittlement, the lips and teeth of predation
predictable unpredictability of miswired killswitch

Child of silence, spouses of spincycle, reanimated daddys
Is this why so many are taught to kneel upon velvet
grains of rice, shards of glass, their own blood and tears
unchosen rituals of severed flesh
other times when calendars are
punctuated by bloodbath and hope

Nightfalls of advent, cooling breezes of evenings
escapes from close calls, and all the coffee you can drink
is this a prayer for us
I want to be your bolt cutter wielding sister
your wild-eyed auntie
your shimmerless teleport superfriend
who packs something far beyond fighting words
Takes more than a touch of glitter
a dead rockstar's leather pants, or a signature move
to transform uncountable legions

But always follow the dosh
buoyancy of privilege, private armies
Commanders In Thieves
Lessons of action figures
outside of joyous homoerotic play
abound with the stuff of the next wounded knee
and so many other domestic battlefields
Propaganda of otherness deftly applied across
bedsheet and blacktop
the crossing of streets and shipping lanes
concealment of deathtoll
raised hoods, raised hoods
and conveniently malfunctioning body cams

No matter where
it will all be applied to places you roam and hide
5G enabling of universal surveillance
precision bunker buster pierces your basement apartment
direct hit on clawfoot tub and toilet
adjacent to central drainstack

Children of sewergas and soma
this is not where it ends
merely a snapshot for your fray-edged album
label it rattling of the old and beat down
to the young and damaged

[An American Dream Says]
[Soon We Will All Be Meat Goo]

Was it spring's heat, slipping into fall
Or simply blush and squirm of my date's discomfort
When my best friend went down on her friend
Bad porn soundtrack stuck on repeat
In back seat of my father's '71 LTD
Gleaming silver with bordello red upholstery
Charlton Heston larger than god above
Framed by pillars of matching plastic trim

Sometimes a concession stand is an oasis
For mosquitoes and a pair of refugees
Where there is no miracle food
Made from high energy plankton
But there are cokes and fries
To share while sitting on the hood
Hard recline of curved glass
Intertwining adolescent fingers

I can't recall if we kissed on that awkward night
Though we made out at other times

Sometimes a date wants her clit licked
And never to see you again
Sometimes not

[American Dreams Of]
[Graduation]

There is cold
Despite the blinding flipbook
Procession of glowing spheres
And conga lines of dislocated bodies
Limbs stutter and twist
Between inhibiting moments of
Consciousness
Spaces in graffiti spread across
Timelines   hale-bop hale-bop cursive
Trailing into black holes of
Memories, sweat, an echo
Of fabric tearing to mark
A new year or to punctuate some
Artifice
Or memory of how water ripples
In light
Is that the sun or
A color dance of bare bulb
Hanging on wire in some lake cottage
Where acid and boy sweat dominate
The playlist
And infinite rebound
Of a block of ghastly green phosphor
Between two frozen lines
May bring a moment's laughter
Sandwiched between autonomic screams
That those boys in their leather, boots, military and police
Future   Are   The   Danger

[In My Runaway Dream]
[I Fall Like Gravity's Infinite Lusts Got Me]

That tractor on a stuck throttle
Run   toward switchbacks and shattered trunks of yellow pine
The way earth smells when it's fresh torn up
They say there's osmium in these hills but all I catch is
The scent of rot and green and near vertical patches of
pavement

And all I want is to lie down across this mountain
Roll my body down to the town by the interstate
Hitch a ride to some magic or meaning
Or any me who is not myself

I come down from the divide
The highway rises to the east
My dreaded direction
But any way you point yourself is ocean eventually
Just a question of temperature
and the hardness under one's feet
If I fell again into the oneness of brine
Floated like the dead do
What of it

[Then I Dreamed & Then I Dreamed]

Who am I?   Where am I?   WTF?   Right?
I woke up in this strange heaven full of coyote.
Full of I can't move.
Full of heat waving out the top of my head.

I won't remember this later, at least at first. And I didn't drink
or drug, I just have a brain that does things on its own. In the
aftermaths of cities, on diets of no sleep, overdoses of social
media, starry skies and the way my ears scream with no sound,
all reveal the rent backdrop of this backwater shared illusion.

They may tell you it's an old joke, those gods of ours may crack
a wry smile, suck off the energy of a quick caress as you and I
check the status of the physical. Sliding between dreams, on
frosty explosions, I kick the thin steel covering of a walk-in's
door. That odor of fresh sawdust and stale dairy would fade as
I drove from my job every Friday to see my first lover, every
weekend when I was not quite eighteen. Fade to peach-scented
shampoo, the softness of a downy neck swirled into my chain-
smoked Marlboro lips. Feed me for my marathon run from
myself, girl. Always running, I'm just around that next corner
or out of my arm's reach. Or maybe one can fall into self, like
the end of a dream, that freefall into waking or onto concrete
face first. When my sneakered feet tangle, I sprawl on my face,
arms raised like some lost ecstatic dancer.

[In Their Dreams I Discover]
[Tuesday's Quest For Respite]

Notes voiced across wire fret and synthesizer key
Arpeggiate a procession of moment and uplift
Echo within an auditorium soon to be demolished

V formation of waterfowl ever shifting over
River valley and reservoir, every dam below a testament
To trickle and the fickleness of wind and cloud
Their love both gentle and scathing

Ticking of a chronometer at the center of the earth
Where the pilots say it is nearly time to leave our orbit
Amidst slowly rising whine and judder of stabilizers
That as little as possible will lie in ruin without
The explicit focus of will and hands
  directing wrecking ball and blade

A diesel engine coughs, clears it's stacks
That new soot and bluish sputum
May birth a debris field where that auditorium
And the gymnasium below once stood next to
Locker rooms that held an atmosphere
Of perpetual pubescence and those preparations
That are said to enhance or to conceal chemical semaphores
Of fertility and lust
Though after all these ages or because of their
Seemingly neverending stretch
Cheeks still redden
And will continue to do so

After all the bricks have fallen
  woe to those who have attempted to stand
Windworn and bone crackle
A Freeze-dried lifetime is at least as worthless as any
Pursuit of the stubborn
  whom others in the midst of their delusion
May call steadfast
  for sleight of hand is most often performed
In the shadow of a darting eye and shuffling feet
The pilots at the center of the earth
  are the only ones who never waver
Nor do time and space afford them such latitude
Their starched and jeweled uniforms reminders
Of their station and their need for surety

The gods allied with monsters
  plus a few ragged and star-stroked
Humans care not for gold nor blood
But only seek the power of redaction
To hold a moment between grasping fingers
And transmute those terrible clock ticks
That their burdens and their selves
May be released to fall lightly
Or topple, thunder, soot, and bluish hazed
Into the embrace of their newfound mortality

Motionless

When the non-moving air
Seeps into a body
It does little good to turn your
Armature of rebar and twisted wire
Upon its side
In search of some tiny glint
Longing for a bit of liberating limelight
Moon's face and conical rays
When the comet comes to guide you
Through sunless morning
Across boundless sea of motionless
Air and frozen waves below
This is how a diaphragm
Refuses to yield to will
Or a pressure differential
This is how Boyle's Law lies broken
Upon the icy tongue and groove
The way stray fingers drift over
Ridges of cold metal that is not steel
Nor does it move like quicksilver
Another poison that may line the veins
And brain matter of the many
Who have paced concrete
And cages clutching a requisition or a bin
Wheeling a cart amidst those damned echoes

Murmurs too human between damned discharge of air hose
And cylinders, the rattle of glass fibre slabs and boxes
Moving from endless conveyors on to shining rollers
Becoming pitted and worn from the weight of days
When a body lies down, decline, recline, a laboring
Retirement minus fantasy of another day or of needs met
This is the taxidermy of life
How to become a prize
That none desires

[Dreams]
[Of A Breathing Effigy]

i've killed myself so many times before
because my faith in death is unshakable
i am but effigy and hollow
borrowed pieces of desert plants
wrapped in sewn scraps of my worn out clothing
ready for the pyre again and a new name
always a new name and never one fully of my choice

i'd say i'm human candle
plus one handful of desert dust
but somehow i keep burning beyond the end

the hollows in my chest are a boundless desert

i was dragged here for being an animated insult
some spirits take that poorly
though they often pass a person off to other hands
just to be free of a foolish bother

in some ending i am simply a top who spins so quickly
that i appear to be still and serene
while simultaneously
being able to see clearly in every direction

i could be a lighthouse
but nobody listened for so long that
in those ways i lapsed into silence

[Dreams of]
[Those Who Came Before And After Science]

When their savior hurtled from the sky
With flaming fingertips and a thousand
Voiced wail   the way acceleration
Multiplys   the impact of vocal folds
and Doppler shift of relative velocity
Still, I swear that I heard the words
For I have touched the demon core
And mastered the mysteries of criticality
Voiced in diminished harmony

And who of those assembled
Would dare call me liar
If my testimony were voiced
Though all assembled may learn
to love their doom rather sooner
than later   doused in a harbor wide
Tsunami and steam of ten thousand dying
Dragons unleashed

Though my lungs were previously
thought to be powder burned and frayed
I breathed deeply of this singular
event knowing that the other witnesses
Would use this day to bolster their sense of surety
and that I may not desire to remain
In this land   besieged by those who believe
themselves martyrs
Or to be touched   anointed by the hand of
Such a foolish god.

The Earth Pilots don't give a fuck and continue to polish
Their gem-encrusted epaulets
A falling god has yet to affect our course
In any discernible way
Despite the ripples one may cast upon the surface

[There Are No Dreamings]
[In These Hills]

My sister's body
Our parent's golden girl
Whom I believed to be my friend
Several lifetimes ago
Is buried on a hill in Jerusalem
A place our mother, an artist
Said had the most beautiful golden light
Late in the afternoons

A city I would have emptied of all
Until only the voices of cobblestones
And some unfortunate birds
Could be heard
Before all was wiped clean
In a blinding flash that will not be gold
And would sadly be a perfectly futile gesture

You can be fearless
I'm not perfect
Really doesn't matter
I'm half gone now
Near ready to head down that river
Kiss some sandy washout like
I slept with it every night since Halloween
And every Halloween before

And there is
No portage
Just what floats on a body supine and rippling
Like some fluid savior
Or the way sun beams
Into glow of a submerged beer can
Golden like the heart that singer man
Kept on searching
Or was it only a trick
Some lost melody found at the intersection
Of dream world and jugular

Let me tell you   child
That I'm well past half gone now
And I've gotten   old

[The Dream Moves]
[One Step Closer]

Does the paper   and the ink matter
When all my pages blew away on desert wind
Like flocks released from prisons
Of twisted wire and bargain aisle 1 by 4s

There is a feel   to a target pistol   all that weight resting
In the curl of my fingers

If I were   a god   or a devil   perhaps I would better
Grasp what chaos can be unleashed
By a projectile of such small caliber
The way a cactus spike, prickly pear by any other name
Feels like my family spitting   deadname after deadname
The abandon of a shooter with a cheat code
How being on the receiving end of infinite ammo
Feels warmer than
Being confined within their frozen memories
How those   adjacent apparitions   believe them selves
To be effectual   while the winds shout otherwise
Even a fool like myself will tell them   *blow up and dry away*
Leave no thorn in your aftermath

Flock released   that heft balances well in my hand
I only need one shot

[More News From]
[Another American Dream]
[Concession Freedom or Fire]

I.
My non-existent eggs
might sell for sixteen or eighteen dollars a dozen

I have no gonads
And have never had ovaries
Was certainly not fit to be a mother
During what would have been my child-bearing years
Though I did adopt a stray cat or two

With age and ill health
constant weariness permeates my life
Impossible to conceal from anyone as perceptive as
a child
or a pet
or a love
All who may feel they have driven me to a state
As natural as water flowing downhill
As natural as when an inferno consumes
Spent earth cracks under weight of sun and season

Often I can lift myself
From the pad where I lie
on my love   the solidity of floor
Sway and stumble to a chair
Where I sit
And type words such as these

My therapist said that calling this
the sunset of my life
Is too defeatist
But I step outside
To meet the gusts that rock my tiny trailer
Put shirts into bucket
Swish my bar of soap
How is this giving up

II.
Do I want to give up

On some days like this
When dampness enters the matrix
that may continue to steady my flesh
And fragrance emanating from the rig
two or three spaces upwind
Punches me square in the face

/when my ears sing jagged melody/
/overstretched cords of broken gaia/
/give voice to a tortured libretto/ my teeth   the choir/
/scream of branching nerves/
/call and repeat/ of let my skull and mandible go/
/freedom song of synapse & breath/
/accordion folds of cortex/ who is that squeezing and pulling/
/digging fingers fumble across buttons and keys/
/is this wheezing arpeggio a death song/
/a final rattling of bellows/
/snowfilled scan   a thousand vacant channels of/
/noise a pseudo-random backdrop that plays across my vision/
/aggregate of sidebands filled with remains of right-wing pundits/
/wireless security cameras/ and garage door opener codes/

How is this worthy of continuity
this that began with photosynthesis
sprouting of flagellum
when life learned this art
In the beginning there was escape   search and destroy
long before mushroom clouds and plumes inescapable
before grids of metal
before frequency became both savior and strict warden
That which is not carried upon the vendor's cart
will always find means to reach   to caress   lasso   or bludgeon
Do you cling to the belief that
trashheaps are somewhere over there
overlooked perhaps by gleaming glass clad towers
monuments to radiant office suites
and hotels   where faucets run rounds of adulterated copper
barely worth counting
but precious to a body's sustenance
in a world that revolves metallic

When I knew youth and entitlement
   I bargained over pennies
      with those who needed them much more than myself
Hounded by such regret
   how can I find rest in the bitter nights of winter
How is this the sunset of my life

III.
I'm tired of my life slamming shut in my face

I hate when I have hope
Especially enough to try jumping through hoops
Transformed into   a desperate chi-dog
After the treat that could be my life
Some pilgrimage less tortured
Less akin to   infinite days in the hole
They rolled a boulder across the escape from the oubliette
Bound weights to my overwrought limbs
Such that they became pillars of leaden fire

What does it mean to gasp life into this relic
Moment by moment
Imagining reach
Dreaming grasp

Is this trance sunrise
Or shattered glaze of
Kiln cracked day

Skyfall draws up dusk
Perhaps a gesture
This   modesty of the dying
Should I fade into static
with skirts held high
Or smother aspiration in layers of blankets
Declare myself guilty of life
of clinging to moments
Supporting illusions of time
and other dimensions
That appear to exist
And lever open what becomes   between the rise and fall
Measures laid down in the signature of rattle
Coda in the key of expiration
Keening against a wind
in the colors of rage and sadness of the weary
Does every click track   footfall   heartbeat   lead to some end
More certain than one in the chamber
Or a witty epitaph
Rubbed onto paper held against the wind of winter
Pencil as phonograph needle scraping up words
perhaps never spoken by the one
whose remains lie here   covered
But more likely the utterance of one who persisted
at least for some interval

Five
This is the forgetting of dreams across generations
accumulation of drudgery
upon the upper moulding of every door frame
It rains down as worn and weary cross
each and every threshold
varnished hardwood tread by ancestors
and blessed black sheep among them
dreamers and queers   in the end often say keep going
try to make your end exceed the roots of your wounds
or cut them open   and let them bleed clean for once
This is your body   this is your blood of your life
these are your tears in your darkest times alone
eat and drink of them   that you may release them
to walk among the world   sprouting word and suture
the prizing open and mending together of flesh and spirit
strange ritual in the woods   and across the plazas
stain the earth and concrete   which is also earth
that multitudes may recall these ways

[Smothered American Dreams]
[Of Pride]

Pubes don't grow out of tiles
In a public women's shower
But maybe you sprung full grown
From a low-flow shower head
Disposable razor and sickening
Fake floral fragranced
Gloop   I guess because that is what it looks like
Contributing to the danger of this curly minefield
You've laid down, enough to blanche the faces
Of a regiment of sappers

Maybe you're excited cause it's pride month
And you want some one to taste your rainbow
In a random hotel room or some other public facility
That you have yet to defile

Dear Pride, I hear house beats and racism
Transphobia and police details
Sometimes we pay for our own imprisonment
At least it's a bigger closet, a place with more space to hide
Sunburned, beer canned, and condomed
Pledge our allegiance to pennies and dearest prudence
This is the same old marching season
White washed and wingtipped across asphalt
Of another great american hangover
I can't even remember which city it was

[Another American Dream]
[Of Parentage]

My mother told me I was born in the wagon of a travelling show
but she loved to tell me lies
She told me she loved me and that I would have a beautiful life
but watch out for communists and queers
except for the one who did her hair

My brain won't leave me alone
It is a bully who only wants my tears
and doesn't give a fuck about lunch money
I carved the word *DESIST* into my forehead but it didn't help
It reads backwards when I look in the mirror

My feet get angry and I don't know why
They still hate me
even when I give them new socks and oil them before bed

Lately my mouth only yawns at the end of winter's short days
I am still infatuated with the nights
even if they are trying to freeze me
Perhaps I will become a plank
some sort of frozen human dessert

I am already seen as a novelty by many
That is about the best an old tranny can hope for

Hope hates me too
but the feeling is mutual
We have both cheated on
each other far too many times

I guess I come by that honestly
My father was a cheater
and would double down on his lies
His brother was also a gambler who would double down for
the thrill of it all

My birth certificate says I was born in a hospital
but it had the wrong name on it
Now it has a different name but it is still a wrong name

No matter how fast I run I cannot
keep up with the speed of change
The rate of change of chance
is the click that the second hand of a cheap wall clock makes
when I want it to be quiet

[Another American Dream]
[Genital Beauty Pageants]
[And Other Spectator Sports]

I have become obsessed with taking better crotch shots
But my clinical   critical   oddly wired   awkward   gray matter
Revolts almost as much as
  the hair I could have sworn I scaped just yesterday
And my disobedient flesh decides to line up flaming trash cans
Threatens to beat me upside my head
  with my own number 4 dilator
Plastic transparent gift
  that keeps on giving me possibly false memories
Of a couple I once knew in some other random timeline
They smiled too happily   acrylic
And when we fucked
I could taste listerine and individually baked nachos

[Another American Dream]
[The Peggy Hill Stomp Porn Experience]

They tried to surgically correct my clitoris
But it retreated yet again
Falling into me
To her place of familiar discomfort
We cohabitate
Forever in exile

My pubic hair is beginning to propagate
Toward my hips
Like yet another invasive species
Sustained by a cocktail
Designed to delay the wasting away of this body
From some combination of mysterious diseases
Or a lifetime of solitary confinement

My feet never obey me
And prefer to turn ugly
So I punish them with the cheapest plastic sandals
Then try to appease them
Alternately lavishing them
With the finest extra virgin coconut oil
And ignoring them completely
They see through my attempts at mindfuck
And despise me

[In My Dreamless Sleep]
[I Pinned You]
[Up Against The Wall]

If we were together   In a polycule
I would nickname it   Texas Death Match
Lights above the ring   Cut jagged cones
Edges of shadow   Milky way of dust motes
Hate filled   Blood family occupy
Folding chairs   Tubular metal barriers
Getting off on judgement   Sucking off
    my residual discomfort
One or another comet looms nearby   Their orbit has
    brought them over
Don't try to take   The top rope, kid
My elevated place   You're still a lightweight
    (even as you grow)
You see there's the words   Unnature Girl bedazzled across
    the back of my robe
Writ in glitter across my trunks   My ass an ageless artifact
Deserving fear and worship   Reserved for
    perpetual belt holders
And iron-clad magic girls   Stronger than the thighs
Of a thousand generations of grandmas   Fed up with
    mothering everyone
    and everything
There's a time and place   Hold your hand close
Fan those cards carefully   But when the bell rings
Everything is aimed at   A count out
Submission   Fly without a ticket or a boarding pass
Land with a crash   The referee always looking
The wrong way   As was ordained by
The shape of   The game itself
Never a winner   Only a payoff

[Dreams]
[Of My Body]
[Of My Life]

How do I bring myself to love this wreckage
When, upon waking each limb seems burdened, paralyzed
And to lift this lattice, expand diaphram downward
Feels an act of handcrank and stubborn
The way exhausted mind resists unconsciousness
Siren's song, cloudbuster gathering dreams

I am void plus water plus dream
Equals wreckage
The way I cleave to unconsciousness
Once touched, attained, once paralyzed
But lines of force, noise and waste perpetually stubborn
Precipitate, I only know how to rain downward

In life unconscious, there is infinite downward
For the fallen, there are falling dreams
No rest for the stubborn
Afflicted with impacted wreckage
Curare blood primed to paralyze
Where is the border wall, frontier of unconsciousness

Where is the love, sweet kiss of unconsciousness
There are only arms that pull me downward
For months my wakeworld arms were paralyzed
Like decades when I did not dream
Like years turn bodies into wreckage
Movement is alchemy of the stubborn

Love is a spell cast by the stubborn
Magic of unconsciousness
Reanimated scrapheap, sheaths and tendons of wreckage
Gaze fixed downward
Scanning for misplaced dream
Often times a mind is paralyzed

When thought precedes a life paralyzed
This is when a world or a city appears stubborn
Chokehold on dreams
Riptide of unconsciousness
Pulls me outward, jerks me downward
Into wreckage

When dreams, fever sweat, paralysis
Enwrap this, my wreckage, immovable, stubborn
In blessed unconsciousness, I descend ever downward

That day I smelled dirt
but it turned out to be blood
　　　- or-
The Epic Of Girl Flesh

Are poems demon-slaying spells, weapons that bring time and memory to heel, leashed and obedient, to be transformed into sublimating pools of burgundy. Does one dare to raise a glass of this rising bouquet of spite and years. Ghosts of the vanquished are only sung of in refrains of pop songs, vapid and cold. The touch of their icy fingers leads me to recall bloodless arteries that fed the curbstones of my shadowed past.

Is it necromancy to raise up highways and misguided loves. The ways that I was borne upon fear's shoulders, balanced between the obvious certainty that I would plummet, kiss concrete with tangle of myself, bid goodbye to the illusion that I might just keep riding above confluence of rock bottom and infinite chasm. Rock bottomless, the way I cast myself again into attempts at grovelling before the feet of ephemeral existence. What can one do when an anthem rings hollow.

Skittering fingers, rebound of scar across tempered silica plains of infinite android. Romance of bone and gearwheel punctuated by bursts of haptic purr. To stroke the glass kitten is perhaps better than rubbing gravestones of those I actually knew. The immediacy of footfalls on graveyard paths. Sunny Saturday morning coffee dates with the deceased before a basement reading of promises, as most assembled scatter across the play field of one more day. Hours counted in green sheaves and copper, heart beats and clenched jaws.

I will always be someone's problem child in their perception or in fact. Shifting images of painted concrete walls, long since bulldozed and filled. Remnants of signs, bullseyed bumblebees, they rattle metallic of civil defense. Was I, that youngster, believed to be a random strike, an accidental discharge of chaos, or a frontal attack on friends and teachers, sunday mass, synagogues, stars and stripes, our america nourished by five cent devil dogs and raspberry cokes, gallons of simple syrup doled out in paper cones, the miracle of weakened virus, hamstrung pathogen in rows of tiny cups, hopes arrayed upon a cafeteria tray. Drink of me for I am sparkplug, striae, smoothness of heartbeat, the way a ribcage rises and falls, tidal volume. Cautiously cloudsurf, shooting curls that never cast themselves spent upon our shorelines.

Pro wrestling is like a new and better fake orgasm. The straight boys eat it up but most won't eat a girl's crotch with the born again fervor they show for well-oiled man muscle or an ice cold Dew. If only they would do you the way they do the Dew. Their tongues seem slightly less lazy, though verbally shackled by the same old lines, fashioned from song lyrics, and threads snipped from less than memorable memes. How do you say hey with all the enthusiasm of Buckley before and after his ascension, under the influence of sweet lady propane, into red-vested angelhood. Loyalty to the heavenly mega-lo-mart but not the heavenly that resides in your clit. Holy nerve bundle branches of Tigris and Euphrates.

It's all about the blood. When the tide turns from umbilicus to succeeding uterus, crash scene of the next generation, intersection of heartsbeat and hours. How does one love you?

Let me count your wounds, you ephemeral crustifiction, all the days invisible, wellspring so-called eternal at the root of world tree and generations runs dry. There is no hourglass to turn as the final grain falls into the multitude. Mothers who are the legions that have tread upon remains of remains ever shifting, starstuff they call and respond, but what flesh can withstand such fire. Certainly my passport is not valid within a foreign gravity well, and daily I am bathed in all which-while came before and will be in this sphere.

Perhaps I'll inhale viable remains of some hitchhiker replicant that coasted in between gamma ray and seagull's wing, a bit of nearly backward-compatible microcode. With every such ending, an opportunistic idiom may seem infinitely executed.

Do we do the loop-the-loop, stack overflow, be in our way unknowable or deftly step and repeat our path, clatter of ten trillion mousetraps snapping, lung wheeze and collapsing synapse, metrics of the rate of change, acceleration of induced degeneration. Degenerate was a word unspoken but pervert was certainly thrown my way, spawning my desire to be plain spoken, to rail against the grasp of entropy. How do I honor tides of generations, when like myself others before felt the weight of you and your shame-filled delusions upon their neck

How do you even talk about such things? You just talk, Sister!
It's kind of like packing. You just pack, and if you're like me in
the day you pack large, rock an appendage of outrageous color,
learn to laugh when the straight moms yell *fake dick!* , just like
when they call my flesh artificial, christen my cunt mystery
hole. I was never baptized by any other than my self, the
severed flesh of old testament covenant a harbinger, like the
act of toppling minarets in 1948 foreshadowed generations of
strife.

All that I am are meaty bits laid bare, new take on a familiar
pâté garnished with sweat, suture bumps, and oil, produce of
some remote grove of trees, coconuts poised upon pliant
minarets that beckon in desert wind, and do not burst into
flame, far too many lives sacrificed on altars of turnstiles,
lipstick, and pencil skirts.

I have often dreamed of that other club, seen faces of the lost
100, imagined snapping Einstein's spine, pixie stick granules of
lightspeed burst over my tongue. Language of event horizon
and angular velocity brings me to that terminus just in time to
snatch those pyros. If I can't get them out any other way,
perhaps I could conceal them in my so-called fake cunt. Could
be that I have a TARDIS in there, or more likely an entire
magical kingdom resides in my mystery hole. No problem! I've
learned to stand a bit of heat in my nomex and kevlar lined
vulva. Yeah! That's right, sweetheart. Finger my button at your
own risk.

[Good Morning, Love]

A half empty can of spray cheese I found on an abandoned campsite
A peppermint tin filled with half smoked cigarettes
Red and clear, an antihistamine capsule, also half emptied
A well-worn disposable lighter that still produces a tiny lick of flame
This is how I continue through this whispering apocalypse

If I turn you on your side, kiss the taste of vomit from your swollen lips
With mine
Will you wake into this holographic mist
Rainbowed with diesel fume and pesticide
Stay-fresh fragrance and paralytic dispensed from a no-drip spout
Take a pull from that well used water bottle that crackles in your hand
Both coated with oxide from a metal floor

Would you allow me to pull you closer
By the lapels of your fatigue shirt
The one you got from that skinny junkie girl
Who always thinks everyone is out to rip her off in trades
Or wants her unwashed ass

This is how the sun rises over the hill
Or I am jerked awake by the slam of a vehicle door
Signifying that someone is out there
When all I want to do is gaze upon the dream of your face
In blue tinged light
Our world filtered by dusty bath towels
Hung over loose sliding windows
That do little to keep away the night time chill

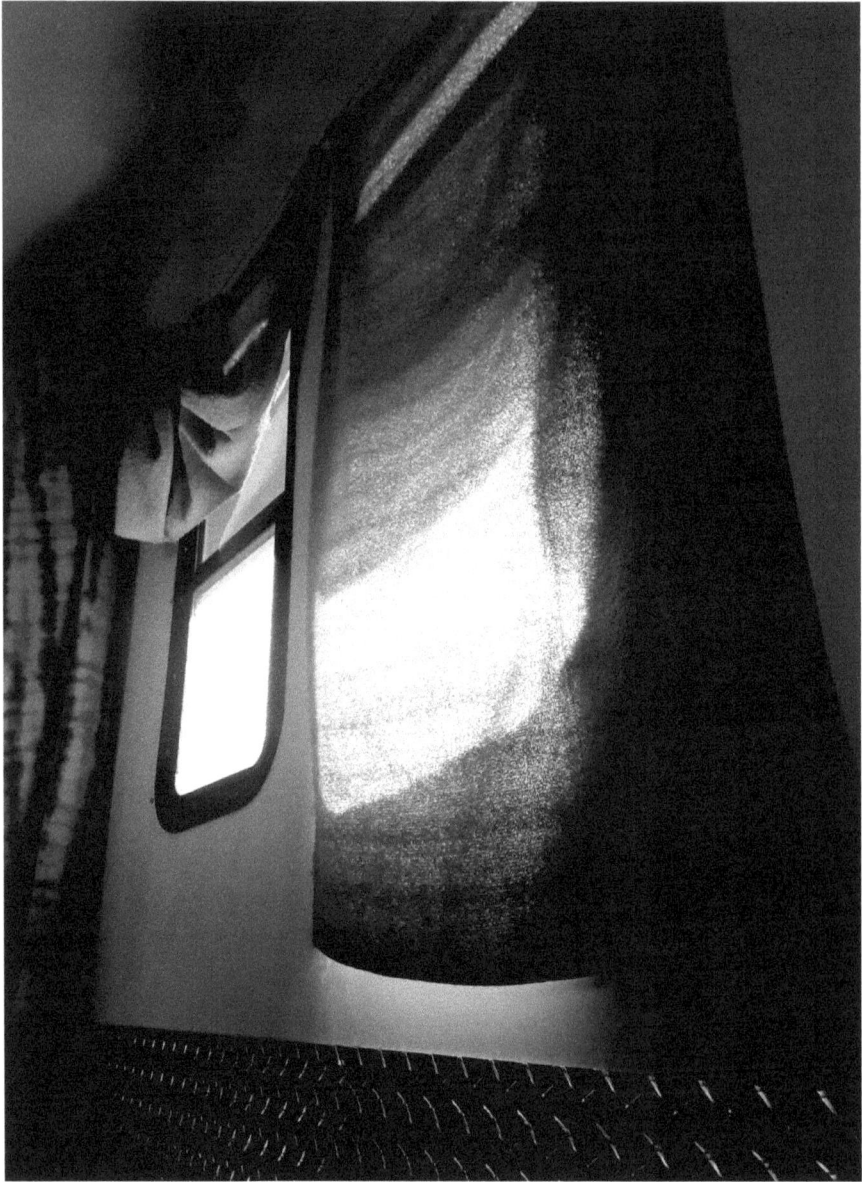

[In My Dreams]
[Call Me Something]

I tread a liminal staircase
Between my broken temples
Path of a pilgrim   called by crack of jaw
How trumpet sings noise and migraine
Amidst ululation of minor Gods

When cacophony reverberates into
Loosely screwed hinges
Spanning gaps between moment and lifetime
The years disassemble
On clouded formica supported by
Stainless steel extrusions
A coffee stained
Kitchen table strewn with
Galaxies beyond number

This is how to inhale
Purchase seconds
Exchange rate unknown
This is how to release
Falling framework
Sometimes there is a window
Or an x-ray   Perhaps an equation
Or a name
Some answer to an appeal   For vision
The way I may phase into being
To satisfy void, vacuum, an upturned palm
This is how to live
Call me something   perhaps
Or cast a shadow to caress
The naked earth

[Final Boss]

My face is always melting under starlight
The immense weight of heavenly assemblage
chants in unison
this is our gift to your cowering self
and her immediate fear of
Discorporation
the disbursement of molecular self
grieving bone and drapes of flesh

Entropy is always twinkling down on me
the way that clouds and dust motes
carry our bits and pieces to prove that
past lives can scatter past light

Infinite few would ever recognize my old faces
or the touch of my hands
and my will

If time is an illusion
why does it create such ever widening gulfs
between memories of selves
stirring at the edges
of waking
or some wandering midnight journey

[Does Vapor]
[Dare Dream]

In any world where I may be said to exist
Under purple sky baked by frenzied orb
In a place where orbits of bodies
And hearts
Know only fidelity
To the love of random
The love of castoffs
The love of roads brought to being by motion
Where we live so purely
In the embrace of the love of leaving
Do I dare utter the words - I wish to stay

Yggdrasil in Starlight

All I see is the way you look upon me / like I've fallen / between worlds yet again/
/as though you may finally / realize / that I am unbound by the serpent's ring/
/the means by which a sphere may exert a grasp on itself/
/for always we are compelled to separate that which we believe is ours/
/from the fearsome touch of void and other/
/on these roads I journey / you are often with me/
/alongside more than you may consciously understand/
/on some days a muse is not so much bathed in aspiration as shod in practical shoes/
/clothed in rolled cuffs / another tramp warrior or stranger to all we may encounter/
/I am ever falling / into juggernauts predominated by fire ice or mist/
/you always blink at me/
/and snap me back into sharp focus

Hydrogen

The fat horses on their patch of pasture
don't care about cars and trucks
bouncing over broken two lane
They ignore the dance of rubber, asphalt
dopplered voices of praise jesus
radio sermons and children fighting for dominance
of the back seat or a parent's attention

The world crawls or does it
balance on a high tension wire
unaware that freefall ends
in the domain of crawling scavengers
that replication was only created for their sake
to be disassembled that it may be left raw again
upon the sand and lifted by the wind

When I remember that I am breathing death
without a trace or flicker of flame within my nostrils
that every word I speak once walked or flew or crawled
over sands and stairways of this Earth
or traversed light-years for this moment
of spittle and wheezing exclamation

Verses fold upon verses
the way that pages are bound and glued
only to become yellowed confetti
This is how we always speak endings
tongues curling and obsessed with
an illusion of the new

The sun Is a ball of hydrogen
Fusing
And not a sphere of burning blood
When it rises

I slide my winnings and my injuries
into a leather pouch I carry on my hip
Define my self by losses
The way you come and go
like seizure and silence
a winter sunday snowfall
and how you trip over lacings
of your own monogamistic patterns
always repeat them from neuron to synapse
That motion as your arm sweeps through air
like clearing a table or a gameboard

I know the game as surely as I know marketplace stalls
spoken languages
the pungency of spices blending
a world sifted over skin, hair and clothing

I know to keep walking, to hitch my pack up higher
like I got the shoulder blades of Atlas, or Tarzan
or some Mother's Mother's Mother before me

For Doug Smode (Written July 2024)

When I walk with the dead man in the desert
Who to so many appeared in such stark relief
As to render all assembled wraithlike and cloying
I don't want to write this   to reveal myself
As poly-obsessessional without a calendar
Without a sense of time or place
A thousand lifetimes painted across starfield
And endless sand dunes

The dead man   dragon-like
Split tongued and split-dicked
Laughs and sings of forests
Hardwoods and blizzards of my dreaming
He speaks in small campfires and lunges
Of loyal and loving canines
This is how to grab something gigantic
Hold it in your palm while shouting
A never ending torrent of   most magical curse words
Before letting it all escape into the love of gravity's pull
Spaces between fingers were born to be wormholes
Portals into infinite freedom

We slacken our pace to grant names
To unknown constellations peering down at
Us between inkstain clouds
I tell him, *I wish I could have done better by you*
He replies, *I know*

Call Me Earthling

I am become polyvinyl acetate destroyer of gray
Illuminator, bringer of bright colors
Divine discount deal   may be a stagnant sargasso sea
bound up in failing myelin
Savior in a coat of many sublimations
Sheathed in back hair and protruding lower lip
Call me animal, Call me box office, Call me profit margin
Call me kapok eater   Call me carpet muncher
I am become
Genesis at crossroads of wet panties and water bed
I am become wellspring & clockspring
The ticket you feel bounding behind rib and
Floodwaters running through temples

Somewhere there are foundations
I am them
I was from the beginning the fundamental flaw in omnipotence
That is fear but will not name itself
Among the billion handles of gods and monsters
Call me thundermuffin
Call me buckskin bound in coonskin cap
Call me perfect bowl of ramen   bullet train
In land of few bullets
Call me tilt of hip   invited brush of lip
I exist in every shadowed corner   tip of every pen
I come to you in darkened hours
I slide through synapse and belly sweat
To sweep away stagnancy of embodiment
Legacy of meat   seemingly packed in three dimensions
Illusory borders of self
That seem all too visible

In the beginning there were simple replicators
So it is in the end
Only the marketing changes
Overlaying a mechanism hidden
In bursting bubble of anti-entropy
You are more than that
Behind veil of carbonation
Above floor jack, amphetamine
On some days a pretty face
An elusive orgasm
A moment's pleasure
A Coney Island in the sky
Fading

How [The American Dream]
Tried to Skullfuck Me on Public Alley Nine-Oh-Nine

(After Human Sexual Response's Public Alley 909 &
Helicopter Helicopter's Sinking Light)

This might be about how our corporate overlords
Don't pay their people enough for a lifegiving trickle
Down into potholed alleyways
Laid out on sunbleached tatter of backseats
The Buddha, skirted with scotch tape and greenbacks
Remains erect upon a fake granite countertop
He dreams of rubbing one out, mummified in gold leaf
and the reverence of strangers
This is How we drift through summer streets on the hunt
Scent of vomit wafting from Central Square storm drains

I cross the river to public alley 9 oh 9
Where jangled jam bounces out an open basement door
Under the record store, dank brick and concrete rooms
Hum of ground loops
Constellations of crossfire
Supernovas shred
Detonations at Mass Ave and Boylston

A passing thought
Who was the last to get railed
on that mattress in the dusty corner
And did anything of value change hands

Do I join the ranks of the devalued
Whose dayjobs subsidise their gigs
Or perpetually couchsurf a circuit of friends
And windowless practice spaces
That mattress again

Man with the hands
That wed quicksilver and concussion
Responds that I know enough to be
In a lot of bands, except

For my intimate knowledge of
How it feels to perpetually lack chops
In every endeavor dear to one's heart and crotch
While all that trickles down is
The certainty that I will
awkward my way out of every good thing
Before it's even started
But accept corporate cubicle subjugation
In hope of remolding my uninsured ass some day
While our nation's an installment plan
Payed in bodies of the undesirable

This is how Rushmore crumbles in twilight dream
How perhaps for one moment my voice will refuse
To catch in my throat the way my mother's did
Except to berate her own

Is accepting that I remain excruciatingly unfuckable
My key to freedom or simply another answer
In some bar room trivia contest

Lay me down on stovetop
Lay me down on softening asphalt
Carry me to somewhere sordid, sober
Time Warp to a doorless stall on Necco St
Rattle slabs of sheet metal, graffiti, and crust
Or back to Public Alley 909
The way my tobaccoburst slabtop bruised my ribs
And cut like a hammer who daydreamed knife blade and
heavenly choir

Where is that hidden harmony caressed
Within the folds of my green stamp catalogue cunt
A solo penned for the clit who likes to
Run and hide from arias in the key of tenderness
Tendon, Synapse
Knuckle, Scar
What does one do with fingers
Who refuse to sing for the sake of the hand
In devotion to cochlea and sweat

This isn't church choir practice
Though sometime afterward
Laid out on sunbleached tatter of backseat
Maybe give me what you got
Maybe I'll call it even
Maybe The Buddha
Skirted with scotch tape
And sinking light
Would like to watch

[another american dream]

My gender is murder...

But who's ghosting or otherwise discorporating
While
In this city I carry a slingshot and a pocket full
Of ball bearings simply to hear the silence before
Impact   the way things may shatter or exhale quickly
Into darkness and occasionally
The sound of rebound or ricochet

In the end everything rolls
In the end everything is roasted over flames
Or coals or swallowed raw
This is how a jaw walks into
A small town
It is offered the choice to speak or to eat
But the unfolding words whisper of moderation
Say never pull on a thread harder than the twinings
Of fingers and verse

Night times fall into wavering lines
The way that an ocean kisses shore
My gender is nonsense
My gender is full moon
I swim naked and with all my clothes on in the same moment
I am also both hunter and hunted

My gender is murder
My gender is murder
My gender is murder
Fuck your theories
My gender is a pile of dead bodies

I trade my ball bearings
For a pocket full of shells
My shotgun life goes on

[In Our Waking]
[We Wander]

We began walking south from Sharm el-Sheikh
Though we had all lost our magics and forgotten
The names of our gods at some time
Possibly in the distant past or maybe in the moments
Before that morning's sun rose to bathe in another
Of the fifty days, of oven and grit that wore away
At my eyeballs and nostrils so that I only saw and tasted
Sandpaper and the remains of my twisted entrails

Two of the other women said they had set out from Dbayeh
The third said that Beit Hanoun had once been her home

I had wandered since before the sea had courted these
Once beaches, unrequited in the way that so many flirtations
Find their end, so it was that the tide fled one final time

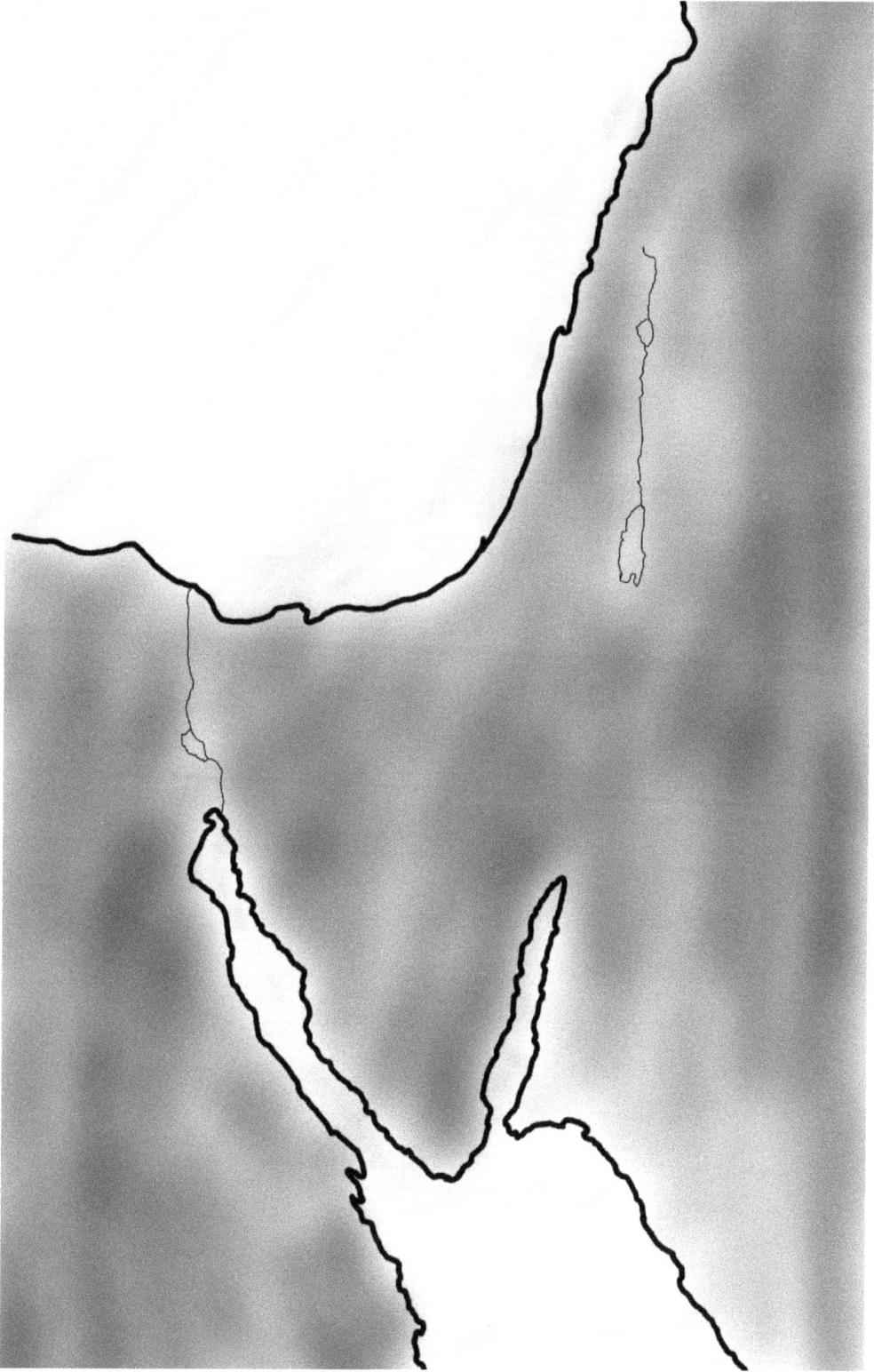

Epilogue :

Wednesday Nov 13th 2024
[Another American Dream Of]
[Happy Days]

Happy days are here again
I tried to run but fear again
I need some sleep but don't know when
Or where or how I'll find my end

They'll confiscate my body
Try to bury me with a wrong name
And none be able to stop them
To deliver me to the flame

Happy days are here again
I tried to run but fight again
We need some grace but don't know when
You know it's us they try to end

They'll take away my body
Try to bury me with a wrong name
And none be able to stop them
To deliver me to the flame

They talk about a covenant
But I'm the one who owns my flesh
I'll strut my stuff like there's no end
Happy days are here again

They try to take the parts of me
I've earned at such great cost
Why don't you just leave us alone
Why don't you just fuck off

I'll gather up my ashes and throw them in their face
Cause we been here forever and we ain't goin away
We'll strut our stuff like there's no end
Happy days are here again
Happy days are here again
Happy days are here again
Happy days are here again

[May we find Darkness and Light in balance]
[May they guide us well]
[May our victories be true and enduring]

Terry Blade is an outsider in more ways than
she's ever been able to understand
A dustpile who tries again and again
to take wing   to transform herself into
something cohesive amidst an ever-shifting reality
and against the backdrop of the ticking time bomb
that is her life

Notes

First, The Meta Notes - These notes are by no means comprehensive. They are simply thoughts that I had while looking through this list of poems. Do not assume that because I mentioned a particular aspect of meaning or one precipitating event, that other meanings or events are not also woven into a piece. Please do not let any of these notes negate your personal understanding of my work. Instead, I hope they enhance, add to your understanding and appreciation.

I also feel compelled to mention that some pieces of this work, from my perspective, seemed to originate in a place beyond myself. I have done my best to retain the meaning, and the spirit, of such work as I have translated it to the page.

I try to come to my writing and editing with the assumption that my readers are intelligent, perceptive, and empathetic individuals. I try my best to not insult you by handing you everything laid out on a platter.

Regarding *After Life Suspended*, and other poems that reference suspension:

I participate in modern flesh hook suspension. I choose to call it a practice, and often a personal ritual, performed within a subculture of our modern society. This must not be confused with cultural suspension rituals practiced within a number of indigenous cultures. Those rites are specific to their cultures of origin, usually closed to outsiders, and likely cannot be properly understood by people who do not have a grounding in the originating culture.

[another american dream] - Is the road an antidote for the ways we are forced to drag ourselves through our daily labor, or is it just another trap, wrapped like so many others, in an artificial fluorescent glow? Hat tip to Doomtree for their ride to the bottom of a pocket, and the bottom of a fifth.

Ricochet (for the vagabonds) - I didn't start out with the intention of putting a Marc Bolan song reference into this poem. Sometimes unexpected connections form, and things just click.

[Falling] - This poem takes, as it's starting point, a certain type of meditation that I used to perform, and then runs with it.

I live in a world of ratchet strap dreams... - At the time I wrote this poem, I did not know that Eric Darby's *Scratch And Dent Dreams* took a bit of inspiration from Buddy Wakefield's poem, *Pretend*. This is actually a good thing, because otherwise I may have been tempted to shoehorn a lemonade stand into *Ratchet Strap Dreams*. The photograph following this poem was taken the morning after I spent my first night under the tarp.

Almighty - It seems that my most direct questions about the nature of divinity, and our relationship to such, often find their way into villanelles.

Shout! Shout to the tiled roofops! - This piece has its origins in one of Valerie Loveland's *Magic Poetry Workshops*.

[Dreams Of] [Returning] - This is based on my personal experiences in the early 1970s, as is the previous poem.

[another american dream] A Bitter Taste - Based on my personal experiences in the 1980s and first half of the 1990s.

[another american dream]
i believed i knew what my life was about   but i didn't - I'm still not totally happy with the title of this piece.

Praise for your collarbones

How you have fallen from heaven, morning star, son of the dawn! - During the time I was writing this book, the character of Lucifer kept popping up everywhere. With my consciousness so primed, I wrote the bones of this piece during a *Magic Poetry Workshop*.

[I don't believe] [I'm dreaming] – My miswired neural network is, in large part, a reference to the fact that I have lived with relatively severe Multiple Chemical Sensitivity for most of my life. It is a major determinant in almost every decision I make. Other ways that I not neurotypical are woven into this piece, and this book.

[Another American Dream] [i tried to wave that big dong]
[but she just called me a fake dick] - The title of this piece refers to an incident that took place when I packed large at a party.

[For Comets Who Orbit] [Formerly Drowning Selves]. [In The Lands Of Asphyxiation] - I won't speculate about the reason, but somehow my writing about spiritual experiences frequently comes out sounding like sex or masturbation.

don't care that it's midnight

Ca-Cha! or [Another American Dream Dies Here] - This and the preceding piece, don't care that it's midnight, were both prompted by a specific incident of harassment in a public women's bathroom and shower. It is many years since I have had access to private facilities.

[this is not a dream] [in the midst of] [Fissure] - This moves through my experiences while I was displaced during, and following the COVID shutdown. It also pulls from encounters, butting heads with trans-exclusive so-called feminists. I'll let the declarations, and challenge at the end stand on their own.

[Propagating The Cuttings Of] [Another American Dream] - Sometimes consciousness grows on its own schedule, while the machine always continues.

[In My American Dream] [All I See Are Dead Children] [But All I Write About Is Bullshit]

Reiteration - This poem was written in the early 2000s, and is prompted by travel, and work that I did in the 1990s.

[A Different Dream] [your average creature of the shadows] [nursing a long-broken heart] [and a rebellious meat suit] [awaits resuscitation] - The ways in which we can put our bodies, and our spirits into each other's hands leave me in awe.

Every day I talk to a ghost - Rage On, Dougie, And Rock That Purple Dress! Heart emojis don't print right, and real hearts pump blood, not ink.

(whatever holds me) (to these places)

[The American Dream Of] [Smasher / Devourer]
[Lays Down By The Riverside]

4:55AM Transmission - In the performance version of this poem, I recite the complete lyrics of the song, interspersed with my lines.

[Another American Dream] [Return Road From A Suscon]

[I Dream My Way] [Across America's] [Four Lane Blacktop] - I wrote the original version of this piece in the early to mid 20 teens, about a trip I had taken a few years before. I performed a major rewrite for this book. I kept the tin can for eight or nine years, and lived in it most of that time. The picture of me in the driver's seat is likely from a time a bit later than this story.

A Priest, a Minister, and a Rabbit walk through my dream
And I praise the Fluffy Bunny for being most wise

[In Last Night's American Dream] [Everyone Was Famous For Three Minutes] [On The Internet] [But Not Me] - Hat tip to City Girl's *Heartbreaker Club But It's Pop Punk*.

[In The Middle Of The Dream] [Everything I Once Craved] [Makes Me Retch] - This is an intentionally broken sestina that I began due to a prompt by Adam Stone for the *Saturday Night Poetry Exchange*.

[Another Dream Of] [Taking On That Sheen] - Another poem that started in the *Magic Poetry Workshop*. This one takes a bit of inspiration from my love of large shiny metal body jewelry.

[Another American Dream] [Some Stillborn Convocation] - A small tip of the hat to Fear Factory's song *Linchpin*. Also a refutation of one viewpoint, as I change the lyric *We see no end to the dream* to *We see an end to your dreams*

Divination - Using hook suspension ritual as a gateway is not without risk. This particular suspension took more out of me than any other to date. The picture is a frame grab from a video shot by Russ Broty that I edited and cropped. It is used with Russ' permission. Suspension was by *Life Suspended*.

After Life Suspended - This poem appeared in my previous book, *Call Me Earthling*.

I lost my faith on the day I met you - A bit of fantasy crashes into reality, after Helicopter Helicopter's song *Please Pleaslle Tito*.

Incarnatus – It is common for Jews who live in communities that have a significant gentile population to be called *Christ Killer*. This is especially true during the Passover, and Easter season, when anti-semetic sermons abound in some congregations. Of course, the old anti-Jew standby films *The Passion of the Christ*, and *Barabbas* are trotted out to throw fuel on the fire. Likewise, in my experience, the taunts were also common among kids, and teens.

Jewish versus Catholic, mostly Irish, gang fights were common during the time of my father's adolescence, and usually took place in Franklin Park, Dorchester. He told me of his involvement only in general terms. Check out the origins of the musical *West Side Story*, originally brainstormed as *East Side Story*.

146

[This Is] [Replica] - The title of this piece is based on the way that Burton C Bell, the lead singer of Fear Factory would introduce the song *Replica* at live gigs. Aside from that, It is probably best to not compare my life or experience directly to the subject of that song, though there are some parallels.

Beauty Regimen - I lived many years in the beautiful but incredibly harsh desert with only rudimentary shelter, and no access to running water.

Practicing Sums - This piece dates from the early 2000s.

[More News from the Underworld] - I originally intended this to be the title piece for a different book.

[Recycled American Dream] [Self Sabotage] [Is] [My Birthright] - This is one of two poems in this collection that takes a bit of inspiration from David St. John's *Lucifer in Starlight*. St. John, in turn, cites George Meredith's poem with the same title via an epigraph.

[Dreaming Of] [The Small] - This poem continues a couple of themes.

[American Dreams of] [Meat Ghost, Most to Toast] - The title is obviously a play on *Space Ghost, Coast to Coast*.

[Another American Dream of] [Rebranding] - The corporate ownership and operation of prisons has remained in the front of my consciousness, partly due to my close proximity to the prison complex in Florence, Arizona for many years. I sought to explore this lineage.

Child - In this case, I was chosen as a suitable messenger.

[An American Dream Says] [Soon We Will All Be Meat Goo] - I doubt that my father's LTD was actually gleaming on the night in question, though it may have been reasonably clean.

[American Dreams Of] [Graduation] - Yeah, I was tripping on that night in 1974 when I played my first game of *Pong*.

[In My Runaway Dream] [I Fall Like Gravity's Infinite Lusts Got Me] - Among other things, this recalls days up on the eastern continental divide.

[Then I Dreamed & Then I Dreamed] - What happens when a not quite 18-year-old closeted trans girl dates a genuinely nice person in 1974, and can't come close to making the pieces of her life fit together.

[In Their Dreams I Discover] [Tuesday's Quest For Respite] - I wrote a lot of this in the *Magic Poetry Workshop*.

Motionless - This dovetails a life of factory work with years of illness and homelessness, living in vehicles, tents, and a metal trailer.

[Dreams] [Of A Breathing Effigy] - I held my own funeral, burnt my then self in effigy, on a winter's solstice day in the Sonoran desert.

[Dreams of] [Those Who Came Before And After Science] - The title is a spin on a Brian Eno album. Much of this was written in a Magic Poetry Workshop.

[There Are No Dreamings] [In These Hills]

You can be fearless I'm not perfect - I do not like the song that I referenced very much, but it holds some truth

[The Dream Moves] [One Step Closer]

[More News From] [Another American Dream] [Concession Freedom or Fire] - I don't particularly love the number four.

[Smothered American Dreams] [Of Pride]

[Another American Dream] [Of Parentage] - I don't know what my mother thought about Cher in the end.

[Another American Dream] [Genital Beauty Pageants] [And Other Spectator Sports] - In the end, I have, over many years, performed my own revisions to my original surgeries.

**[Another American Dream]
[The Peggy Hill Stomp Porn Experience]**

[In My Dreamless Sleep] [I Pinned You] [Up Against The Wall] - This may not be the best contrapuntal, as the two sides are not particularly disparate. It is the only poem I have successfully completed in this form.

[Dreams] [Of My Body] [Of My Life] - Another venture into form.

That day I smelled dirt but it turned out to be blood - or- **The Epic Of Girl Flesh** - While some of this may have come from beyond, much is grounded in personal experience. The whole string of riffs toward the end rises from speculating about what could I actually change if I could travel back in time for perhaps a day or two with only my current knowledge and understanding of past events.

[Good Morning, Love] - How do we live, and love in the midst of my beautiful toxic wasteland.

[In My Dreams] [Call Me Something]

[Final Boss] Hat tip to Doomtree's *Final Boss* for hands & will

[Does Vapor] [Dare Dream]

Yggdrasil in Starlight - Another poem that takes inspiration from David St. John's *Lucifer in Starlight*.

Hydrogen - More musings on the cycle, again via the Magic Poetry Workshop.

I slide my winnings and my injuries into a leather pouch I carry on my hip - Another nod to Doomtree's *Little Mercy* for winnings and injuries.

For Doug Smode – We never know what it's like, 'til we do

Call Me Earthling - I wrote this long after my book, *Call Me Earthling*, was published.

How [The American Dream] Tried to Skullfuck Me on Public Alley Nine-Oh-Nine - Public Alley 909 runs behind the stores at Mass Ave and Boylston Street in Boston, across from what is now the Berkeley College of Music building but was, in the 1990s, the homongous Tower Records store. The buildings in front of 909, especially on Boylston Street, were full of music stores. Daddy's was on Mass Ave but around the corner was Jack's Drum Shop, DJ Price, Cambridge Music, and Looney Tunes record shop which was a hub for local student and street life. Mass Mental Health Center is now further down the Fenway but I think they also had some buildings that were closer, back in the day (not certain on this). As to inspirations, Human Sexual Response's *Public Alley 909*, and Helicopter Helicopter's *Sinking Light* both deserve mention here.

Necco St, first the site of The Mad Hatter disco, and more importantly, later the site of The Channel rock club, no longer exists in the same form. The Fort Point Channel district was re-developed into an upscale innovation area. The Channel was humongous, wild, and often kind of scary. Definitely missed by many.

[another american dream] My gender is murder...

[In Our Waking] [We Wander]

Epilogue :

Wednesday Nov 13th 2024 **[Another American Dream Of] [Happy Days]** - Very loosely based on the tune of Mission Of Burma's *Sing-A-Long*, played at dirge tempo

Playlists

At the Gas Station, there is always music and video playing, though the speakers may be a bit frayed, and the screens splattered with a record of events that would baffle most forensic investigators. These are the favorite playlists of the two overnight shift employees who work the most hours, have to put up with the most shit, and kick the most ass to survive.

Janky Jenny's Playlist [URL] = bit.ly/dickpills1

Little Mercy performed by Doomtree, featuring Dessa, and Cecil
Fuck The Pain Away performed by Peaches
I'm Moving On (written by Hank Snow) performed by Steppenwolf
Spaceball Ricochet performed by Marc Bolan (early demo)
Great Big Meaningless performed by Helicopter Helicopter
Foggy Mental Breakdown performed by Steppenwolf
Burn It Down performed by Sims
Securitron (Police State 2000) performed by Fear Factory (w/lyrics)
Down By The Riverside performed by Sister Rosetta Tharpe
Heartbreaker Club But It's Pop Punk performed by City Girl
Please Please Tito performed by Helicopter Helicopter
Replica performed by Fear Factory
Transmission performed by Joy Division
Beacon performed by Doomtree (live on KEXP)
Gravity performed by Nuno Betttencourt (live in Portugal 1998)

Public Alley 909 performed by Human Sexual Response
  (10th anniversary reunion 1990 at The Channel Necco St Boston)
  props to Subterranean Video for this
Sinking Light performed by Helicopter Helicopter
Salaam performed by Mosh Ben Ari & Sheva
[Another American Dream Of] [Happy Days] ... Terry Blade

Ball And Butt Bustin Beths's Playlist [URL] = bit.ly/dickpills2

Pretend We're Dead performed by L7
The Bends performed by Doomtree (Audiotree Live)
Type performed by Living Colour (live)
Cosmic Dancer performed by T Rex
Renegade performed by Steppenwolf
Bolt Cutter performed by Doomtree (Live on KEXP)
No More Pennies performed by Starcrawler
Seether performed by Veruca Salt (Glastonbury '95)
Self Bias Resistor performed by Fear Factory
  (MTV Headbangers Ball Live)
Down By The Riverside performed around the world Featuring
  Grandpa Elliott, Preservation Hall Jazz Band,
  and Congolese Choir of Grace
Fallen Angels performed by Nuno Bettencourt
The Last Ride performed by Todd Rundgren
  (Live From Daryl's House)
Coney Island Baby performed by Lou Reed

Empty City performed by Three Friends
Final Boss performed by Doomtree (Audiotree Live)
Pound performed by Human Sexual Response
   props to Subterranean Video for this
The Afterworld performed by Helicopter Helicopter
Don't Forget You performed by The Stupid Stupid Henchmen
Witchitai-to performed by Jim Pepper with guests
   Billy Cobham, and Larry Coryell
Salam Ya Falastin – performed by Siedd (Official Nasheed Video)

Notes: I had originally planned to end this playlist with Witchitai-to. That is the vibe and style I was shooting towards in the arc of this playlist. But when it came down to it, there was no way that I was about to leave Siedd's words and message on the cutting room floor. So I decided to give him the final word in this playlist.

After reading my work in this collection, and listening to the final verse of *Salam Ya Falastin,* I could not help thinking about how we who have been raised in a world of nationalism, militarism, and violence, have inherited and absorbed the language, idioms, and imagery associated with those ways of approaching the world and each other. It is my sincere hope, though our roads may be bloody, that all of us, as artists, and members of the human family can cast off those ways of thinking, so that we may find better ways to express our aspirations and dreams.

Acknowledgments

In my first book, *Call Me Earthling*, I acknowledged the communities, venues, and people who supported me during my formative writing, and performing years, in addition to those currently in my life. The bulk of this book was written and revised during 2024, and early 2025. I especially want to acknowledge those who've been here for me during those times.

Dee Birch
Gabriel M Falcon
Alicia E Goranson
Johnnie Xel
Adam Stone
Diane Ellaborn
Tony Amato
Magic Poetry Leader, Valerie Loveland & The Magic Writers
Saturday Night Poetry Exchangers

Special Thanks To:

The Someday I'll Learn To Love Writing Poetry Group
Adam Stone, Berent LaBrecque, Kelly J. Cooper,
Sue Savoy, Valerie Loveland

Thanks to some of the old ghosts and others floating around the pages of this book: Laura, Valerie, Amy, Mark, Karen

All Possible Love to Jeff Taylor for your encouragement, unique voice, and all those amazing Friday nights.

www.ingramcontent.com/pod-product-compliance
Lightning Source LLC
Chambersburg PA
CBHW042346030426

42335CB00031B/3473